DELIVERING EFFECTIVE TRAINING SESSIONS

Geri E. H. McArdle, Ph.D.

A FIFTY-MINUTE™ SERIES BOOK

DELIVERING EFFECTIVE TRAINING SESSIONS

Geri E. H. McArdle, Ph.D.

CREDITS
Editor: **Sara Schneider**
Layout and Composition: **ExecuStaff**
Cover Design: **Carol Harris**
Artwork: **Ralph Mapson**

Printed in the United States of America

English language Crisp books are distributed worldwide. Our major international distributors include:

CANADA: Reid Publishing Ltd., Box 69559—109 Thomas St., Oakville, Ontario, Canada L6J 7R4. TEL: (905) 842-4428, FAX: (905) 842-9327

Raincoast Books Distribution Ltd., 112 East 3rd Avenue, Vancouver, British Columbia, Canada V5T 1C8. TEL: (604) 873-6581, FAX: (604) 874-2711

AUSTRALIA: Career Builders, P.O. Box 1051, Springwood, Brisbane, Queensland, Australia 4127. TEL: 841-1061, FAX: 841-1580

NEW ZEALAND: Career Builders, P.O. Box 571, Manurewa, Auckland, New Zealand. TEL: 266-5276, FAX: 266-4152

JAPAN: Phoenix Associates Co., Mizuho Bldg. 2-12-2, Kami Osaki, Shinagawa-Ku, Tokyo 141, Japan. TEL: 3-443-7231, FAX: 3-443-7640

Selected Crisp titles are also available in other languages. Contact International Rights Manager Suzanne Kelly at (415) 323-6100 for more information.

Library of Congress Catalog Card Number 92-073847
McArdle, Geri
Delivering Effective Training Sessions
ISBN 1-56052-193-7

This book is printed on recyclable paper with soy ink.

PRINTED WITH SOY INK

PREFACE

This book is for trainers or anyone who is still learning the craft. It is especially for technical experts who must make a presentation or train others in their area of expertise but have no experience in presenting.

With this book as your guide, you will acquire the skills and confidence needed to make you a competent presenter from the outset. Using the exercises, you will be taken, step-by-step, through the detailed stages of presenting your knowledge to your audience. These steps will include:

- Setting up the environment
- Using your materials effectively
- Encouraging participation from the toughest audience
- Dealing with problems that arise, either with the group or with individuals in the group

Geri McArdle

ABOUT THIS BOOK

Delivering Effective Training Sessions is not like most books. It has a unique "self-paced" format that encourages a reader to become personally involved. Designed to be "read with a pencil," this book offers exercises, activities, assessments and models that invite participation.

The objective of this book is to teach the basic techniques of delivering good training presentations. Understanding and practicing these techniques will help a reader improve the quality of his or her own presentations.

Delivering Effective Training Sessions can be used effectively in a number of ways. Here are some possibilities:

- **Individual Study.** Because the book is self-instructional, all that is needed is a quiet place, some time and a pencil. Completing the activities and exercises should provide valuable feedback and practical ideas for self-improvement.
- **Workshops and Seminars.** This book is ideal for reading prior to presenting a workshop or seminar. With the basics in hand, the quality of participation should improve, and more time can be spent on concept extensions and applications during the program. The book can also be effective when a trainer distributes it at the beginning of a session and leads participants through the contents.
- **Remote Location Training.** Copies to use for self-study can be sent to personnel who cannot easily attend training sessions.
- **Informal Study Groups.** Thanks to the format, brevity, and low cost, this book is ideal for "brown-bag" or other informal group sessions.

There are other possibilities that depend on the objectives, the program, and the ideas of the user. One thing is for sure: Even after it has been read, this book will continue to serve you well as a ready reference and reminder about the fundamentals of delivering quality training presentations.

CONTENTS

INTRODUCTION vii

PART I ABOUT THE PRESENTATION 1
- Conscious Confidence 3
- Fears and Fantasies 6
- Creating the Event: Gathering the Facts 10
- Developing the Presentation: Organizing the Material 13

PART II REHEARSING YOUR PRESENTATION 25
- Writing the Script 27
- Rehearsing the Presentation 32

PART III IT'S YOUR SHOW 41
- Setting Up the Room 43
- Room Layouts 46
- Mechanical Details 49
- Meeting and Greeting: How to Get a Leg Up 54
- First Fifteen Minutes: Success or Failure 56
- Breaking the Ice 58
- Administrative Issues 67

PART IV THE USE OF VISUAL AIDS 69
- Delivering the Content 71
- Selecting Presentation Aids 72
- Creating Overheads 76

PART V MANAGING THE SHOW 83
- You Are in Charge! Encouraging Interaction 85
- Avoiding Fatal Flaws 89
- Focusing on Your Audience 91
- Getting—and Keeping—the Ball Rolling 97
- Time Considerations 102
- Final Closing 106
- Feedback and Evaluation Forms 108

APPENDIX 111
- Presentation Development Model 113
- The Case Study 118
- Role Play 120

ABOUT THE AUTHOR

Geri E. H. McArdle, Ph.D., is a successful human resource manager, educator and consultant, with a diverse background of experience in both the private and public sectors. This is reflected in her credibility and popularity in publications.

Dr. McArdle is the Outstanding Faculty Member of the Year in the department of Business Administration and Management at Johns Hopkins University and is currently a fellow at the Philosophy of Education Research Center at Harvard University.

Her broad experience includes management positions in General Electric Company and the United States Senate, and administrative positions at Marymount and Cazenovia Colleges. Dr. McArdle has been a consultant for the past ten years with AT&T, Bourroughs, Marriott, Burger King, the Xerox Corporation, the Department of State, and the White House. She is a contributing editor for the *National Society for Performance and Instruction Journal* and the *New Dimension* (Distributive Education Clubs of America), a publication that is received by every high school student in the United States.

Dr. McArdle has written several books and numerous articles. She received her doctorate from Syracuse University.

Dedication

To Phil Gerould, Crisp's publisher, because he made me write this book for him; and Dr. Janette Wright, president of BayPath College, Longmeadow, Massachusetts, for the inspiration she gave me. Also, to Karla Nguyen at Crisp, who provided the gentle prodding that kept me, and this book, on track.

I also want to thank Len Nadler, professor emeritus, George Washington University, Human Resources (and the father of HRD); Gaylen Kelley, chair, professor emeritus, Boston University, Instructional Media; and Cliff Baden, Harvard University Graduate School of Education.

Finally, to my daughter, Briget McArdle, the geologist, who has grown up to be a most wonderful human and talented teacher/researcher and protector of the environment; and my mom, Geri Huebach, who always goes the extra mile for everyone!

INTRODUCTION

What Is a Training Presentation?

A training presentation is any organized activity designed to bring about change in an employee's on-the-job skills, knowledge, or attitude. Its purpose is to meet a specific need.

- *The presentation may be designed to help an employee acquire a new skill.* Skills are psychomotor abilities: the capability to operate a computer, to use a copier, to listen effectively, to write good business letters or to supervise a staff. Skills are actions that can be acquired and observed.

- *The presentation may be designed to provide an employee with additional knowledge.* Knowledge is cognitive ability; it is what an employee understands and can apply to his or her job. Understanding the mechanics of market research or knowing the principles of accounting are examples of the knowledge necessary for certain jobs. Knowledge is less quantifiable and observable than skills.

- *The presentation may be designed to affect an employee's attitude.* You cannot teach ''attitude,'' yet attitude is an important factor in the learning process. Attitudes are in the affective (feeling) domain. As a presenter, you may generally accept that how people feel about what they are doing and about the organization for which they work affects their performance.

How Should You Use This Book?

This book is your SURVIVAL KIT. Use it as your personal map to guide you through the unknown journey of preparing and delivering effective presentations.

If you take the time to think about these ideas and techniques, and to work your way through the exercises, you will have gone a long way toward becoming someone who can teach a group something new and useful. You may even have an influence on their attitude toward their work—and life!

P A R T

I

About the Presentation

CONSCIOUS CONFIDENCE

There is no limit to what you can do, as long as you believe in yourself. Successful presenters, first of all, know themselves. Based on what they know about themselves, they develop their potential, their own style, and their self-esteem. Self-esteem is a combination of:

- Self-knowledge: "This is who I am."
- Self-confidence: "This is what I can do."
- Self-worth: "What I can do and say are important."

In this age, when prospective presenters may be tempted to compare themselves with actors of 30-second TV commercials, it pays to learn how to be effective.

To be effective, you must first of all be conscious of your personal style. Personal style is the way you interpret, organize and "package" your topic. Conscious means being aware of your biases, attitudes and language choices; never speak over the understanding level of the audience nor underestimate your audience, and never say anything that you would be embarrassed about if it got in print! You are unique—and valuable in your uniqueness—and you can make a unique contribution.

Let's take a look at the Personal Style Checklist to help you assess your style.

PERSONAL STYLE CHECKLIST

There is no question that winners are individuals who step outside their comfort zone, who take risks with a well-defined purpose in mind. However, to venture outside your "comfort zone," you must understand the boundaries you have established.

Here is a checklist to determine your present comfort zone. Make notes on each point in the space provided.

- [ ] What are you comfortable doing in front of, or as part of, a group?

____

- [ ] What actions or situations are outside your comfort zone?

____

- [ ] When speaking to people: Will you prefer to lecture? Or do you prefer to have a dialogue with your audience?

____

- [ ] Will you like standing in one place? Or do you like moving around?

____

- [ ] Will you depend on a lot of well-planned instructional media? Or are you spontaneous in your use of media?

____

- [ ] Will you need pre-developed flip charts or overheads to guide your presentation? Or do you use the flip chart sparingly?

____

- [ ] Will you need your presentation to be in a script? Or do you work from an outline?

____

- [ ] What tone and voice tempo do you use? Slow and deliberate, or fast and flowing?

____

- [ ] Will you be an animated speaker? Or a quiet lecturer?

____

- [ ] What style of dress do you prefer? Informal or formal?

____

If you decide that you would like to make some adjustments to your style, go easy, put one foot in front of the other. Adjust your style gradually, taking small steps toward change, yet remaining in your comfort zone.

EXPECTATIONS

Your goal as a presenter is to have an impact on your audience. Research indicates that success or failure in making a presentation is caused more by mental attitude than by mental capacity.

Athletes who train for long periods of time for a specific event, such as the Olympics, plan their physical and mental preparation so that it builds and peaks at just the right moment—the moment of their performance. You must do the same in preparing for your presentation.

You expect your audience to be interested in your topic. The audience expects you to know what you are talking about, to have some experience to share, and to be enthusiastic about presenting.

To achieve your goal and the audience's goal, concentrate on communicating worthwhile ideas in order to help others, not on making an outstanding personal impression. Polished words and fancy phrases are not substitutes for a good idea, sincerely and simply expressed. You want your audience to learn something and, in turn, you may learn something from them!

Hint: All participants look for two things when they attend a presentation: First, "What's in it for me?", which means that in preparing and presenting your topic, you must reinforce the payoff for participants if you are going to achieve the impact you want. Second, participants expect to be able to transfer their new knowledge back on the job. That means keeping the focus and spotlight on the participants as much as possible.

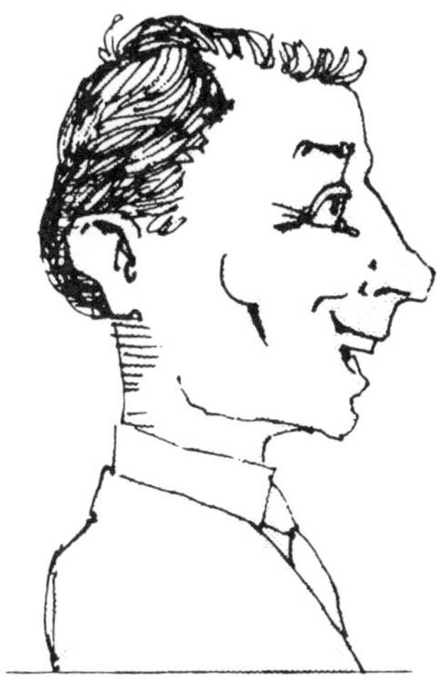

FEARS AND FANTASIES

We all have faced or will face a situation that provokes fear. While we all strongly prefer not to be put in these situations, statistics prove that no one has ever died of the fear of making a presentation. Let's look at the four greatest human fears:

1. Fear of failure, which is actually the fear of rejection. In the case of a presentation, we fear being rejected by the audience and/or by our peers.

2. Fear of success, which is actually guilt. We feel guilty that we are successful when others are not. Or, we feel guilty that our presentation was successful and neglect remembering that we worked hard at ensuring its success.

3. Fear of catastrophic danger, which is the built-in ''fight or flight'' instinct. This particular fear causes the typical physiological changes of increased heart rate, sweating and anxiety. This fear is so instinctive that it triggers these over-reactions to even minor dangers.

4. Fear of the unknown, which is actually associated with the fear of change. Although change is an inevitable process of life, we do not naturally like it and certainly do not welcome change with open arms. As humans, we seek to maintain predictable patterns of behavior, and therefore, change is to become different and is sometimes feared.

Remember, fear is natural. Handling fear correctly can serve as an energy boost to your presentation. Here are some tips for using nervousness to your advantage:

- To feel brave, pretend you are brave already.

- Concentrate on the subject of your presentation and get your mind off yourself. Self-preoccupation is a major cause of nervousness.

- Plan to enjoy yourself. Do not call your feelings fear; call them excitement.

- Avoid caffeine and, especially, alcohol.

- Do isometrics while waiting for your introduction. Curl your toes inside your shoes to release nervous energy.

- Concentrate on your breathing. Do not do deep-breathing exercises—you may pass out. Instead, concentrate on breathing rhythmically.

MANAGING FEAR CHECKLIST

Fear is best managed by controlling the material you must present. In preparing your presentation, first limit your topic to one specific idea. Second, select specific material suited to that limited purpose. Third, arrange your material, your illustrations, examples, facts and statistics in a coherent order.

Once you have organized your material, ask yourself the following questions:

☐ 1. Am I familiar enough with this topic to hold a dialogue with the audience?

☐ 2. Is my material organized to express my ideas clearly and concisely?

☐ 3. Is my message simple and sincere?

☐ 4. Is my material organized keeping the audience in mind? Do I know what they need to know? Want to know? And, what would be nice to know?

Hint: If the opportunity exists, you might also want to visit the presentation room well ahead of time, when it is empty. This will help you to imagine yourself actually giving the presentation while you are preparing it on paper and in your mind. Once you are ready, you could even try giving part of your presentation before an ''empty house,'' so that you can at least feel comfortable and familiar with the setting.

NEGATIVE FANTASIES

Fear manifests itself in negative fantasies. Negative fantasies produce a little inner voice that tells us that we cannot do something, or explains why something will not work, or suggests reasons why the audience will not like us.

Although these negative inner voices make sounds which appear to be logical, in most cases your negative fantasies are not logical projections of future events and will probably never happen. However, the negative inner voices do happen to most of us, and we must overcome them.

The way to overcome these negative fantasies is to be well prepared to make your presentation. Preparation is a good defense for countering the inner voices. You can also use visualization techniques. Let's give this technique a try.

First, think of the worst thing that could possibly happen while you are making a presentation. Next, put this negative fantasy into proper perspective. Putting the negative fantasy into perspective means asking yourself two simple questions: ''How likely is this to happen?'' and ''What will it mean to me if it does happen?''

Here is an example:

My presentation is so bad that the audience stands up and walks out en masse.

The first question to ask yourself is: Is this situation very likely to happen?

Answer: No. Experience suggests that an audience will tolerate even the more irrelevant or boring presentation. The reason for this tolerance is that, as a society, we have been socialized to be nice and to be polite.

The second question to ask yourself is: If the audience did leave, would this incident ruin my career?

Answer: No. Yet it may take four to five good presentations to re-establish your credibility.

Here are two more examples of negative fantasies, and suggested resolutions.

Example One: You have memorized your entire presentation, which consists of all new material. Just as you are about to open your mouth to begin your presentation, you become distracted because the light in the overhead projector has just blown out; subsequently you forget everything!

Solution: As bad as this seems, you can make some appropriate remark using the situation as a teaching point, rather than as a disadvantage. For example, tell them unexpected events do not necessarily mean that schedules have to be changed—improvise and go on.

Example Two: You are explaining or clarifying a point. You turn the page of your flipchart to write down the next point, and your mind becomes blank when you find there is no more paper.

Solution: It is best to defuse this uneasy situation by ''calling its bluff'' and writing directly on the cardboard until you can replace the paper.

Hint: Each time you make a presentation or overcome an uncomfortable situation, it gets a little easier.

Exercise

List two possible presentation mishaps. After each negative scenario, describe a simple way to ''call its bluff,'' or to transform it into a teaching situation.

1. Presentation Mishap: ______________________________

____

Solution: ______________________________

____

2. Presentation Mishap: ______________________________

____

Solution: ______________________________

CREATING THE EVENT: GATHERING THE FACTS

Before starting to prepare your presentation, find out as much as possible about the situation you will be in before actually facing your audience. You will have to call (or write) the person who asked you to give the presentation to obtain some of the information.

There are certain facts you *must* know for all presentations, but some information applies only in certain situations. You will not be able to tell exactly what will apply to your presentation until you are far along in preparation; to avoid having to call repeatedly and say, "Look, I forgot to ask you before, but what about this and that . . . ?" you will want to get as much information with one call (or letter) as you possibly can.

ABOUT THE PRESENTATION

Date, starting time, and **length** of the presentation are essential factors.

Three more factors about your presentation are (1) **topic,** (2) **purpose** and (3) **result.**

► **Topic**—The topic must be stated clearly. Your assigned topic might be anything from "health" to "the stress class on Friday." You could probably talk about the stress class without too much trouble, but where would you start talking about health? You could not possibly tell any audience all about health. Discuss the topic with the person who asked you to speak, so that it is limited to what can be covered in the time allowed.

► **Purpose**—The purpose of your presentation will be either to *inform* (provide information) or to *persuade* (inspire action). You may have a purpose in mind, but if not, ask the individual who asked you to speak if he or she had a specific purpose in mind. The purpose—stated as either to *inform* or to *persuade*—will be an important factor throughout your preparation.

► **Result**—The desired result of the presentation depends on your purpose. There are three possible desired results:

If your purpose is to *inform,* the desired result is for the audience to . . .

1. *Be able to talk about it:* they will know enough about your topic to go out and tell others and answer questions, or

2. *Be familiar with it:* they will know only enough to ask logical questions and sit in on discussions of the topic without feeling lost.

If your purpose is to *persuade,* the desired result is for the audience to:

3. *Take a specific action.*

> *Hint:* The audience should already know how to do the action. For example, they know that stress management is positive; the problem is to persuade them to actually sign up for the program.

PROGRAM SEQUENCE

You should know where you fit in the program and who will introduce you. If you are not the only speaker, you should determine how your presentation is related to other presenters.

ABOUT THE AUDIENCE

- **Name**—You may need to refer to the people in the audience as a group. If you want to antagonize them, just call them by the wrong name! Don't call a systems programmer a technician, for example. *Learn names quickly* and something about the culture of the organization.

- **Occasion**—Why have they come together? Just to hear you? Or for some other reason, such as to get an education, to serve the public in some way, to improve relations between schools and parents? Use the occasion in your planning; relate it to the purpose of your presentation to keep the audience listening.

CREATING THE EVENT: GATHERING THE FACTS (continued)

► **Knowledge of Topic**—Some members of the audience may never have heard of your topic. Sounds unbelievable? It seldom occurs to us that somebody has not heard of our special projects! Or some may only have heard the word that labels your topic but cannot recall anything about it. On the other hand, some people in the audience may already know enough about the topic to talk a little about it. Even if you have all three levels in your group, you should be able to talk at the right level for the audience to understand you.

► **Number**—How many people will be there? Attendance should be stated in numbers, not, for example, as a "large group." To some, 20 is a large group, but some think it takes 100 to be a large group. Know your audience.

ABOUT THE SPONSOR

► **Name**—Who wants you to give this talk? If you know the sponsor's name, you can tell the audience how pleased you are that their organization—or leader—asked you to speak. This will establish rapport and credibility.

► **Techniques to Avoid**—Some sponsors do not like certain lecture methods, such as role-playing or seated speakers. Some do not care what you do as long as you get the message across. If there are any lecture methods that your sponsor does not like, avoid them. Ask before you start planning your program.

► **For Assistance**—Some sponsors will not be able to help you much, but if yours can, you will need not only names but also phone numbers and addresses. A name is useless if you cannot find the person to go with it.

► **Summary Okay?**—If the sponsor does not object, hand out a brief summary of your presentation after you have spoken. This will help the audience to retain what you have said. If they are very interested in your topic, the summary will be treasured; if they are only mildly interested, the summary may be just the thing to develop a greater interest.

DEVELOPING THE PRESENTATION: ORGANIZING THE MATERIAL

SETTING AN OBJECTIVE

Adult learners insist on knowing the whole picture at the beginning of the presentation. If you do not have a clearly stated objective—written out—then neither you nor the audience will know the destination you have in mind.

Although the objective should be used to guide you in preparing the presentation, it must state what the audience can do as a result of the presentation, *not* just what you will do in the presentation itself.

You will either *inform* or *persuade;* the *audience* will either be able to *talk about* the subject or *take* some related *action.* Therefore, your objective will be twofold: it will state not only what you will do, but also what the audience will be able to do.

Set an objective so you can teach to that stated objective. It focuses the content and gives the participants and trainer an automatic evaluation component. Objectives are the beginning and ending points of presenting your training material.

DEVELOPING THE PRESENTATION: ORGANIZING THE MATERIAL (continued)

Examples of Objectives

Look at these examples. Notice that Objective II limits the topic to material that is relevant to the audience. While both objectives are twofold, in Objective II the relationship between what you will present and what you want your audience to be able to do is much clearer than in Objective I. Make your objective as specific as possible.

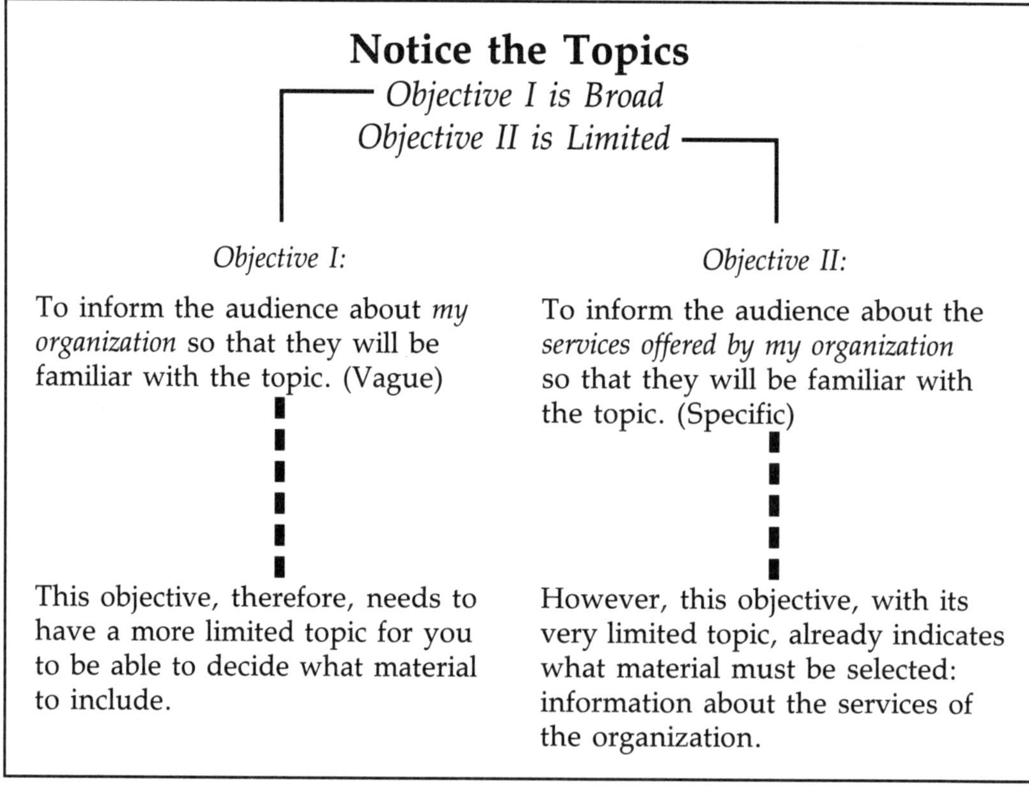

CHOOSE A TITLE

Your sponsor might suggest a title; if not, you will probably have to make that decision.

When you are developing your outline, you may think of a catchy phrase to express your objective. For example, a presentation whose objective is to persuade the audience to attend a stress management program could be titled "Stressed Or Not To Be Stressed?" Or simply, "Effective Stress Management."

OUTLINE THE BODY

Once you have set your objective, you must decide how to reach that objective by using four general organizational steps:

1. Limit the topic (if necessary).

2. Select an approach.

3. Select a pattern (or sequence) in which to present the material.

4. Select a method of presenting the material.

DEVELOPING THE PRESENTATION: ORGANIZING THE MATERIAL (continued)

1. Limit the Topic

The objective includes your topic. The topic tells you what material you must cover, and the objective tells you how detailed your presentation must be.

Let's look again at the two examples of objectives on page 14, compare the topics, and see how we might go about selecting categories of material to include in the presentation.

Objective I could be restricted by these ''limitations'':

- Services (or products) offered
- People in the organization
- The organization table (organizational structure)
- History of the organization
- Physical layout (space) of the headquarters buildings, field offices, etc.
- Purpose of the organization
- Procedures (in the production of one or more products or services)

Notice that one of the limitations on the topic for Objective I is ''services offered,'' which is the already limited topic of Objective II.

2. Select an Approach

Now you are ready to consider an ''approach'' to the presentation. There are many possible approaches, but we all know the six that writers consistently rely on: who, what, when, where, why, and how. Let's consider these approaches in terms of our limited presentation topic, ''services offered.''

- **Who:** people who provide the services; departments or parts of the organization that offer services
- **What:** the services themselves (limitations are also approaches)
- **When:** services offered in the history of the organization (when they began)
- **Where:** places where services can be obtained (such as at headquarters or field offices or even room-by-room)
- **Why:** reasons for offering specific services
- **How:** procedures for obtaining the services, or procedures involved in supplying the services.

3. Select a Pattern

Because "approaches" and "patterns" are so closely related, your approach could easily determine the most logical pattern (sequence) for your material. Let's consider our examples in more detail and see how your approach could determine your pattern.

APPROACH	POSSIBLE PATTERNS
Who	Top to bottom of the organizational structure
What	Known to unknown (from familiar services to those unknown to the audience)
	Frequent to infrequent (from those most often rendered to those least often rendered)
	Problem to solution (from a problem the organization faced in providing a service to the solution found)
When	From the founding of the organization to the present
How	Procedural (step-by-step)
Where	Directional (from north to south or east to west)
	Part to whole (field offices to headquarters or room-by-room)
Why	Problem to solution

Note: All these examples of possible patterns can be reversed—"unknown to known," "infrequent to frequent," "whole to part," etc.

The *patterns* shown on the diagram on page 19 are not the only ones for each *approach.* It is perfectly all right for you to talk about "what" in a "part to whole" pattern, for example, or "who" in a directional pattern (people's locations) instead of the organizational structure.

DEVELOPING THE PRESENTATION: ORGANIZING THE MATERIAL (continued)

4. Select a Presentation Method

Now that you have selected your approach and pattern of organization, you must determine the best method of presenting the material to the audience. Here are several methods from which to choose:

1. **Series of facts:**

   This is the most common method of presentation. The speaker states a fact and then supplies information to back it up. This method is suitable if your objective is for the audience "to be familiar with" your topic.

2. **Series of comparing (or contrasting) statements or questions:**

   This technique is often used in "to persuade" lectures. It is a way of presenting both sides of an argument to the audience with a double-barreled sentence.

3. **Series of questions:**

   You might want to ask questions and:

   - Give direct answers (and then provide the proof).
   - Provide proof and let the audience draw conclusions.
   - Prompt the audience to give the answers, especially if your objective is for the audience to "be able to talk about" your topic.

Important Factors to Consider

LIMITATIONS	APPROACHES	PATTERNS (sequences)	METHODS OF PRESENTING
People or organizational table	Who	Top to bottom (of organization)	
Services or functions	What	Known to unknown Frequent to infrequent Problem to solution	State facts
Time	When	Founding to present	Compare and contrast
Physical layout	Where	Directional Part to whole	
Reasons or purposes	Why	Problem to solution	Question and answer
Procedures	How	Procedures	

SUPPORT THE MAIN POINTS

Now comes your chance to gather support information for your topic. You will want to get all sorts of information. Your audience must be kept awake and interested, so dig out a lot of facts, in a variety of forms. Consider the possibilities!

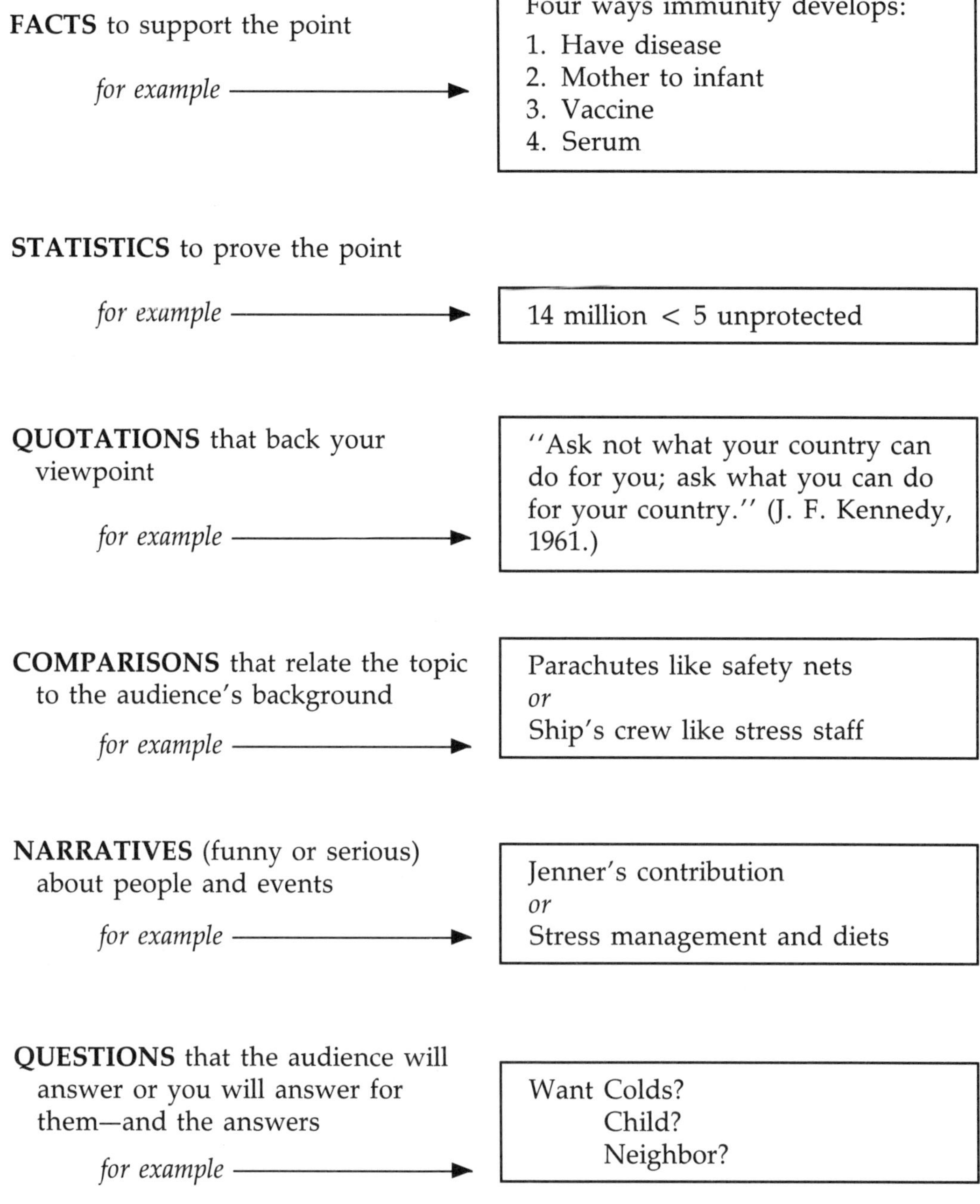

Keep this four-item list in mind as you select a method of presentation and write your main points:

- ☑ Main points should include all material needed to reach the objective (or the objective as limited by the approach), but should *not* include unrelated material.

- ☑ Main points should be numbered in the order in which they will be presented. (This is your pattern.)

- ☑ Each main point must be in the form of a sentence, and the sentences must be of the same type—statements, commands, or questions. (This is your method of presentation.)

- ☑ The best lectures have no more than four main points. (But if you have trouble here, go ahead and write out more than four; condense later.)

Double-check the main points. Are they really independent of each other? Can two or more be combined under more general headings, such as functions, classifications, longer periods of time or bigger steps? Try that, to see if you can condense them to four.

RULES TO REMEMBER

Just as there are rules to keep in mind when you select your main points, there are also some rules to remember as you gather material to support those main points.

Rules are designed to help you. You want to stay on the road you selected. These are your highway markers; they may slow you down a little, but there is always a limit to how fast you can go safely.

Rule 1.

Support material should be in the form of *cues*, not sentences. Why? If you wrote out information word-for-word, you would get stuck with those phrases, and your lecture would lose freshness and variety.

NOTE: Put in as many cues as you think necessary; the more lectures you give, the fewer cues you will need.

Rule 2.

Exception to Rule 1. Quotes must be copied word-for-word, like the original, but in quotation marks. And write down the source! (It is a good idea to put each quote on a card, which you can hold up as you *read* it during the presentation, saying, "as JFK said . . .")

Rule 3.

If your objective calls for the audience to be able to talk about the topic, they must talk about it during the presentation. You can use questions, forcing the audience to give the answers, but cue the correct answers for yourself!

Rule 4.

Stay on the technical level of the audience. Aim in general for the majority, but include examples for both the lower and higher extremes. When in doubt, aim for the lower levels. Better to be too simple than too complex.

Rule 5.

Try to suppress thoughts about presentation aids that now creep into your mind, but if you cannot, make brief notes on them. We will go into detail about these support aids later; concentrate now on what you will be *talking* about.

Note: If you do not have time to discuss technical material adequately, go ahead with plans to present it in the form of a handout to distribute at the end of the presentation *or* when you are discussing it (keep the audience from reading while you are talking about something else).

Rule 6.

Write down all numbers—equations, formulas, complex amounts. Round off large numbers (for example, $4.5 million will mean more to the audience than $4,544,972.26).

SUMMARY

Once you have all of these cues and quotes written down, it is time to select and organize.

FIRST, estimate how much of that material it will take to fill 70 to 90 percent of your talk time. Do not bother to rehearse it; you will do that later. Just make an estimate.

SECOND, pick out the material you want to use. Another reminder: you always want to keep the audience eager, so think of them when you are selecting material. Combine and delete information, and get more if you do not have enough. Use what you think will have the greatest appeal and will offer the most variety, but be sure it relates closely to the objective.

THIRD, put the support-information cues in order for presentation. Rewrite, if necessary, or number your cues in order. Support material should be in the same sequence as the main points.

P A R T

II

Rehearsing Your Presentation

KNOWLEDGE

WRITING THE SCRIPT

Preparing your presentation means thinking ahead. You have spent a lot of time planning, researching and organizing your presentation. Now is the time to test your knowledge by writing out your script. This is essential for establishing your focus, your topic sequencing and your timing. Additionally, once you develop this mental ''storyboard,'' you will be less likely to wander and lose your train of thought.

Prepare the Introduction

The introduction to your presentation serves four definite purposes:

1. To acknowledge the person who introduced you

2. To gain the attention of the audience

3. To motivate the audience to continue listening

4. To give an overview of the entire presentation

WRITING THE SCRIPT (continued)

Let's go over the four purposes that your introduction serves.

1. Acknowledge the Introducer

Write his or her name down so you will be sure to get it right. You can just say, "Thank you, Mr. Such-and-Such," or you can get into more detail at the time of the presentation, if you want to say something about his or her introduction of you.

2. Get the Attention of the Audience

It always helps to have an opening gambit to catch and hold the attention of the audience long enough for you to get into the main part of the introduction. Make sure, however, that it goes with your topic and is not just a gimmick. You can use an aid if you want to.

3. Motivate the Audience to Continue Listening

Once you have gotten the audience's attention, it is time to apply the topic to them so that they are eager to hear what comes next. They can be pulled to the edges of their chairs by a presenter who talks in terms of their hopes and dreams, finances, job, home life, social position, health, government, recreation or children. Any topic can be localized to the specific audience.

4. Overview

"Overview" means summary. It should include a statement of the objective or a summary of the main points—or both. It should tell the audience when they may ask questions (during or after your talk) and if you will hand out a summary at the end of your presentation.

Hint: If your purpose is to "persuade," you may want to be a bit sneaky and not tell the audience your objective, especially if they oppose your views and you do not want to give them a chance to build up strong mental defenses. In this case, you could mention the main points as one-word areas to be discussed.

There are three important guidelines to follow when preparing the introduction:

✓ **The introduction should be written out completely.**

You can outline the body, but the introduction should be written out word-for-word for your protection. If you have trouble with those butterflies, and your mind goes blank, you will have the words in front of you, and they will keep you on the road to your objective. By the time you finish the introduction, the butterflies should be gone.

✓ **The introduction should take 5 to 15 percent of the speaking time allowed.**

It must be long enough to hit the high spots, but not be a major point of the speech itself. You have your main points—the introduction should get the audience ready to receive them.

✓ **The introduction should be written clearly.**

The introduction should be written on the level of the group in the audience least familiar with technical aspects of your topic.

The introduction serves as a contract with your audience. A good philosophy to adopt is:

- Tell them what you are going to tell them
- Tell them
- Tell them what you told them

Write out a one- to three-sentence acknowledgment for an upcoming speech.

____

____

____

____

____

____

____

PREPARE THE CONCLUSION

Once you have written out your introduction, you can plan the end of your presentation.

The three rules for the introduction apply to the conclusion:

1. It should be written out in full (so that you can end dynamically and not fade out as if you were not sure how or when to stop).

2. It should take 5 to 15 percent of the speaking time allowed.

3. It should be directed at the lowest-level group in the audience.

Note: It is all right to use aids here too, BUT be sure to evaluate them.

When you conclude your presentation, you will go through three steps—or maybe just two:

1. Summarize the Presentation

Use your main points and some of your support material, but DO NOT add any new material. You will have finished the body of your presentation by stating your points and supporting them, and the conclusion should be a summary of that body, not an addition to it.

2. Remotivate the Audience

A few hard facts that apply personally to the audience and their daily lives will give them more reasons to be glad they heard you. If you want them to reduce stress, urge them to protect themselves with their diet and exercise.

3. Write Out a Concise Closing Statement

Your remotivation device may be a concise closing statement, but if it is not, you should develop one. It should be compact and pointed enough to be remembered when the rest of the presentation has been forgotten. It should be a one-statement summary of the presentation that applies to the specific audience.

Here are some examples:

DO SAY . . .	DO NOT SAY . . .
• "So remember—buy health now or pay later."	• "Thank you for listening." (The audience should thank you for your time and imparted knowledge.)
• "Protect yourself and your children with vitamins."	• "I hope you heard what I said and will come to the clinic for your shots."
• "Avoid faulty objectives in your courses—seek precise training objectives."	• "Any questions? If not, I guess that's all I have to say."

REHEARSING THE PRESENTATION

Have you ever heard a presenter drone on and on with words no one else can understand? If so, you probably promised yourself never to listen to him or her again; you do not like wasting time with someone who does not speak your language.

''Does the presenter care enough about us to bother to listen to him or her?'' You have probably asked yourself this question about the ''too technical'' presenter, but it could also be asked about the presenter whose half-hour presentation consumes a full hour. The presenter has not bothered to rehearse, and to an audience, timing can be as important as content.

Your rehearsal will serve two purposes:

► **To check your terminology to be sure it fits the audience's vocabulary**

Consider how much the audience knows about the topic. While you rehearse, jot down any words you use that you think the audience might not know. Define these words at the beginning of your presentation.

► **To time yourself**

Present each part of the presentation (introduction, body, conclusion) and watch the clock. Write the time for *each part* on the outline itself so you will have it later; you will be asked to use it again.

Timing cannot be checked if you lean back in your chair and let your mind wander over the presentation. For one thing, you think faster than you talk. Since you must imitate the actual presentation situation as closely as possible, get yourself a clock, a pencil and a lectern if you will use one at the presentation. Set up all your presentation aids. (*Talk out loud* and use gestures—and do not let your aids stand idle, either.) Practice your entire presentation and record below how long each section takes and your total time.

________ 1. Read the introduction. (You will not want to read it during the presentation unless your mind goes blank.)

________ 2. Talk through the body of the presentation.

________ 3. Present all aids.

________ 4. Read the conclusion. (You will not want to read it during the presentation unless your mind goes blank.)

________ 5. Write down the total time for your entire presentation.

Revise Your Outline

You will be revising your presentation for two things—vocabulary and time. Since vocabulary revision is the simplest, let's get it out of the way and then tie the presentation into a bundle timed neatly for delivery.

You should have jotted down the words you thought might need some explanation. If the new words come in the introduction, rewrite it to include definitions (unless you are using those terms to arouse curiosity). If they come in the body, just write a **cue** to yourself on your outline. You should not have any new words in the conclusion; that would be introducing new material. If you do have new words there, *revise the conclusion* to leave them out.

PLAN FOR EMERGENCIES

You were given a specific time to fill with your presentation, and if you are like most presenters, you feel that if an emergency comes up, YOU will not be the one asked to change your speech. You are a guest; the person inviting you could not be rude enough to flip the welcome mat on you at the last minute!

But Ms. or Mr. So-and-So is not being "rude" when she or he asks a speaker to shorten a presentation because the governor of Utopia or the chairman of the board of directors comes in and wants to say a few words, or because the business meeting is extended. Even in a classroom you never know when someone you want to introduce to your students might stop by. If this happens, you will HAVE to adjust by cutting your speech short. Remember, a "timely" presenter is a respected presenter.

Will you ever need to make your speech longer? Of course! You might talk faster when you give your presentation than you did in rehearsal, or the person who introduces you may "present" some of your supporting material by giving an example that you expected to spend five minutes on.

You should be prepared for such emergencies. If they occur and you are not prepared, you will feel foolish fumbling around, trying to readjust your presentation; if no emergencies happen, all the better. You will not have lost anything, but you will have gained security from knowing you were prepared to give both the audience and the sponsor as much as or more than they expected.

✓ To prepare for a **DECREASE** in time:

Make notes to yourself on the outline you already have, using any note system that is easy for you. Mark the support material you will **keep** in the body if your time is cut to 75 percent. Then put another mark by the material you will **keep** if time is cut to 50 percent. (*Hint:* You should not drop main points or any of the introduction or conclusion.)

✓ To prepare for an **INCREASE** in time:

Go back to the pages of notes you made when you were preparing the body of your presentation and pick out the support material you decided to eliminate. List the support material for each point separately and in sequence; then put some special symbol (maybe a plus sign) on the outline to tell yourself when to pick up the additional support if you need to fill more time.

PREPARE FOR QUESTIONS

If you will be answering questions or if you are part of a panel, then you should do some special planning.

Sometimes question-and-answer sessions are the ''fun'' part of the presentation. You get a chance to really communicate, to know that your audience is eagerly listening. BUT . . .

Some presenters want to pass out when the questions are passed up to them. They speak for their organization or about a specific subject without preparing for obvious questions because they think they know their subject perfectly. But it is not easy to think of precise, nontechnical words to give a perfect answer when you are standing in front of a sea of expectant faces, being bombarded with questions.

No speaker can prepare ahead of time to answer every question that might be asked, but EVERY presenter should prepare ahead of time for questions in crucial areas—especially the policies of the organization or difficult topic areas for you.

The less experience you have as a presenter, the more preparation you need. To prepare for questions, you will go through four steps:

1. List **AREAS** that might provoke questions.

2. List **QUESTIONS** that might be asked in these areas.

3. Write out and polish your **ANSWERS.**

4. Make a **NOTE** to yourself to ask for questions **before** the conclusion, so that **you** can end the question period with your prepared conclusion.

PREPARE FOR QUESTIONS (continued)

Common Question-Provoking Areas

- Areas that involve organization policy
- Areas that even you, an expert, find complex or difficult to explain
- Areas that have aroused public interest (shown by newspaper or TV coverage)
- Areas that have stirred up controversy (within your own group or between your group and others in related fields)
- Areas that have special meaning for this particular audience.

Your Answers

Write out answers to any questions that demand more than a ''yes'' or ''no'' answer. This means anything you can think of that someone in the audience might ask—and remember, somebody is curious about each of those areas!

- Write out your answers in full, *word-for-word,* as you will give them.
- Include an *example* or anecdote in each answer.
- Review each answer for:
  - New terms that need to be defined
  - Conclusions that need to be supported
  - Statements that might cause misunderstandings
  - Logic
- Revise answers if necessary.

WRITE A SUMMARY

Check to see if your sponsor objects to your distributing a summary to the audience. If it does not, you *should* prepare one—especially if your objective is to bring the audience to the ''be able to talk about'' level or to persuade them to do something.

A summary should contain the title, all of your main points and the most important support material. You have already selected the most important support material when you selected the material to retain if your time is cut to 50 percent.

Write your summary.

WRITE A SUMMARY (continued)

Survival Tip #1—Coordinating the Program

Every program you present should be viewed like it is your first program, because the feelings that you experience facing the group for the first few minutes are similar to those you experience when you present for the first time. However, remember that the participant will have feelings too, and they are important to address.

If your pre-program activities were intended to set the stage, your program activities should be intended to sustain the action and keep things going smoothly. Here is a structure that should help you manage the process:

First Hour

✓ Introduce yourself.

✓ Have the coordinator open the program and state the goals and objectives.

✓ Cover administrative details.

✓ Allow five minutes for personal introductions.

✓ Have each participant interview his or her neighbor and introduce each other to the group.

✓ Have each participant state his or her personal objective.

Presenting the Material

✓ Introduce the program model (learning objectives, content and process).

✓ Summarize the learning.

Closing the Program

- ✓ Go over the objectives of the program.
- ✓ Briefly review each major session.
- ✓ Ask the audience to complete evaluation forms.
- ✓ Make sure each person has your telephone number—invite their calls.
- ✓ Thank them.

(See the Appendix for a Presentation Development Model to use to design and fine-tune your program.)

After the Training

- ✓ Clean the room.
- ✓ Collect the extra handouts and material.
- ✓ Complete all administrative forms immediately.
- ✓ Write a letter to the guest presenter and/or sponsor.

> *Hint:* This is an exhaustive list that will help you accomplish your task professionally. Pay attention to the list—make it a part of your presentation format.

PART

III

It's Your Show

SETTING UP THE ROOM

The size and shape of the room, the seating arrangement, and your location in relation to the audience are critical factors to know before you prepare your presentation. Following are some important room setup basics.

► **Is the room properly lighted?**

Effective communication, enthusiasm, inspiration, or motivation of an audience is impossible in a dimly lit room. You must be able to see the audience, and they must be able to see you.

► **Does the room have cool, fresh air?**

A room that is too warm, with stale air, will put your audience to sleep—especially after a meal. Cigarette smoke also has a bad effect, especially on the nonsmokers. Try to ensure a nonsmoking policy in the meeting room, or at the very least, set up half the room for no smoking. And make sure that adequate clean, cool (but not too cold) air is circulating.

► **Is the speaking area neat and professional, with no distracting clutter?**

The place from which you present is your ''personal space,'' and your audience will judge you by its appearance.

For your next presentation, ask yourself what kind of communication you want to take place. There are two factors in deciding how to arrange your room: (1) **the audience**—are they senior managers or first-line supervisors; a large group or a small group; corporate or academic? And (2), **the method**—are you going to give a straight lecture or use the group process method; use a great deal of multimedia or no media; make it ''hands-on'' or purely observational?

YOUR WORKSPACE

The last thing to consider in room arrangement is the presenter's workspace. Your workspace is a reflection on you as a professional. Most participants expect you, as the center of attention, to be organized, calm and in control of your materials, your equipment and your workplace.

When you arrange your personal space, try to:

1. Set up a separate table for handouts, on the side of the room or near the entrance. Stock the table with extra materials, pencils and notepaper. Locate this table away from your space, keeping your work area free from clutter.

2. Use a separate table for the overhead projector. The table should be wide enough to hold your transparencies, a master copy of your script, and the student workbook. Avoid using a small table for the projector. Small tables tend to look ''overcrowded,'' and the materials appear to be messy.

3. Put your notes where you can easily see them, but your audience cannot. This will make your delivery seem more spontaneous and ''live.'' If you are not using a lectern, try to make sure your notes are not placed too low or far away. This will help you avoid breaking eye contact for long periods when you need to look at your notes.

> *Hint:* If possible, print certain key lines of your notes in **bold** or LARGE type so that an occasional, quick glance may be enough to keep you going.

MATERIALS CHECKLIST

Review the checklist below and determine which of the materials you will need. Do not count on the sponsor having these materials readily available for your use.

	Packed	Delivered	Set Up
Flip Chart	☐	☐	☐
Extra Paper	☐	☐	☐
Markers/Chalk	☐	☐	☐
Extra Pencils	☐	☐	☐
Notepads	☐	☐	☐
Name Tags	☐	☐	☐
Workbooks	☐	☐	☐

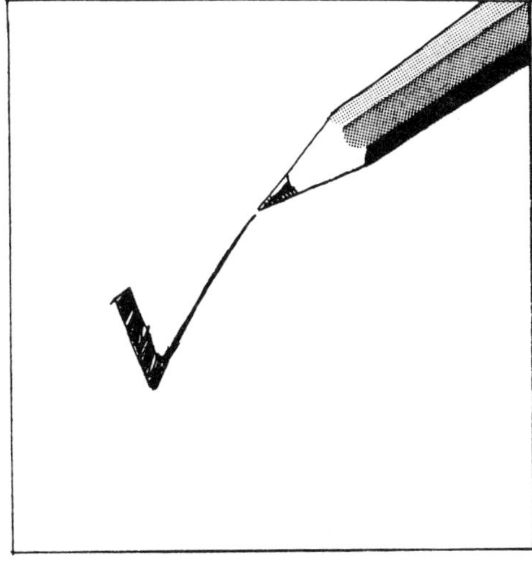

ROOM LAYOUTS

Ask yourself what kind of communication you want to take place, then plan your room arrangement accordingly. (*Hint:* Visit the room well in advance, or call ahead to see what options you may have.) Let's look at several possible room arrangements.

Theater/Classroom:

If you will be speaking in an amphitheater with fixed seats, you will not have much choice. If the location is to be in a room with movable chairs and tables or desks, you will obviously have more choices. "A" shows a standard classroom arrangement, one that fosters communication only between the presenter and the group. "B" shows an altered classroom arrangement, one that improves the opportunity for eye contact between participants and makes things feel less regimented. This arrangement may also allow you more room to move "into the group," if you are so inclined.

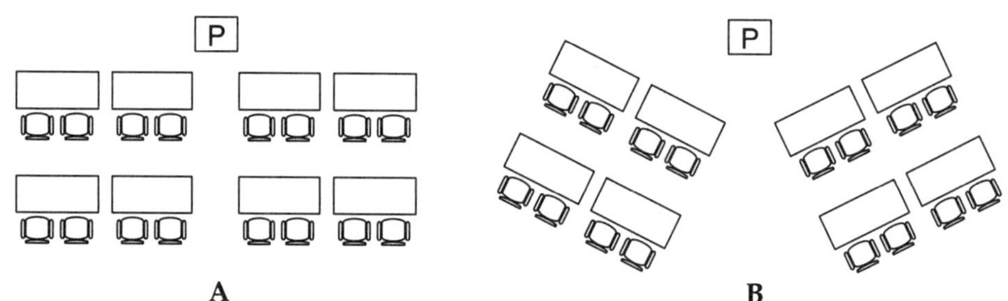

Conference Table and U-Shape:

In a U-shape configuration, participants lose the sense of being part of a large, anonymous group. This layout can be used for groups of 18 or fewer. Making the three sides of the U roughly the same length will increase communication and participation.

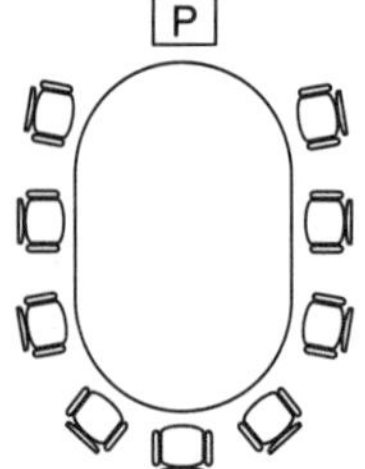

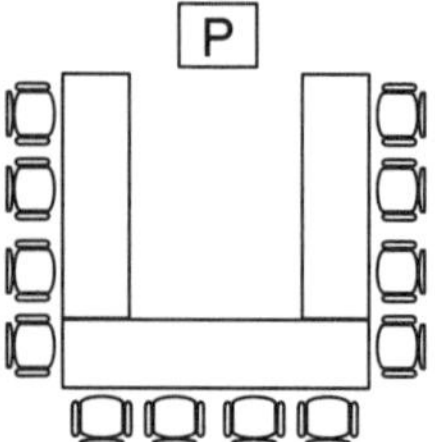

Rounds:

By seating people at only one side of a round table, you allow seating for about four people (assuming 6-foot rounds), with the open part of the round facing the visual aids and the presenter. This plan allows participation in small groups, sharing with the larger group, and interaction with the presenter. If you do not have round tables available, a similar arrangement can be accomplished with rectangular tables with two or three chairs on each side of the table.

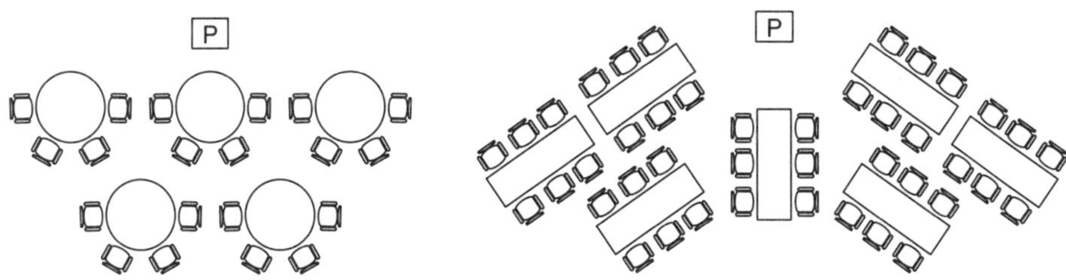

> *Hint:* Whatever your set-up, be sure participants can see you and your visual aids without craning their necks. Otherwise they will quickly lose interest and start making some of your negative fantasies come true!

ROOM SETUPS—PROS AND CONS

Add specific pros and cons based on your own field and presentation style.

Theater Style **Pro** • Good for very large groups • Maintains control	**Con** • Limits discussion • Not good for all visual aids
Classroom Style **Pro** • Everyone can see the visuals • You are the focus of attention • You can move into the groups	**Con** • Creates a "lecture" atmosphere • Not very conducive to interaction within groups
Conference Table Style **Pro** • Establishes a formal atmosphere • Structured	**Con** • Can be used for small groups only
U-Shape Style **Pro** • Everyone can see the presenter • Presenter can walk among audience • Encourages dialogue with presenter • Good for use of all types of visual aids	**Con** • Difficult for small group work • Limits number of participants
Small-Group Style (Rounds) **Pro** • Encourages dialogue among group • Creates informal feeling • You are the focus of attention	**Con** • Difficult to manage side conversations • Takes more time because of interactions within groups

MECHANICAL DETAILS

Using the Overhead Projector

Now for some hi-tech tips on equipment. Select a projector table of ample size. Make sure you use a table large enough to hold the projector, plus an ''in'' and ''out'' stack of transparencies—the stack you are going to use and the stack that is created as transparencies are used. You can place yourself at a real disadvantage by having a table only large enough to hold the projector. Think about other materials you may want to use as well. Will you be using marker pens? Are there other pieces of equipment you may want to place on the same table?

Now let's look at the care and use of a screen for the projector.

- Screens should be at least 42 inches off the floor. Optimum visibility can be achieved by placing the screen in a corner and angling it toward the center of the room. This allows you to write on the projector stage while facing the audience.
- Tilt the screen forward at the top or back at the bottom. If the projector beam does not meet the center of the screen at a 90 degree angle, ''keystoning'' image distortion will result.
- Use a matte surface screen. Beaded screens intensify light reflections to viewers in the center of the room and dull the images for people at the sides of the room.
- Use the 2 × 6 rule to match screen size with seating. The distance from the screen to the first row should be equal to twice the width of the screen; the distance from the screen to the last row should be equal to six times the width of the screen.

Limiting Distractions

The click, click, click noise of turning the projector off and on is a distraction. Here is a solution the author found recently with the help of Ed Jones in Rhode Island:

- Trim a piece of cardboard or a file folder so that it is about 11 inches by 11 inches. (The normal stage on an overhead is 10 inches by 10 inches.) Tape two or three pennies to the top of the cardboard. Now slide the cardboard under your transparency. Move the cardboard down as you reveal your information; the pennies will keep it in place without your having to hold it. When you are finished, slide the cardboard up so it completely covers the lighted stage. Remove your transparency and place the next one on top of the cardboard. You have eliminated the distracting light and the clicking!

MECHANICAL DETAILS (continued)

Using the Flip Chart

A flip chart can be your best friend. It can help you make your teaching clear, can clarify "fuzzy" concepts or can simply be a recording device to make sure that everybody is on the same track.

When presenting and using charts as the main visual, you can write information, reminders, or key points lightly in pencil on the chart. During the presentation, you will be able to read these notations, but they will not be visible to the audience.

The problems with flip charts are presenter-imposed. For example, do not talk to the flip chart. If you record on the flip chart, hold the chart with one hand and write facing the audience on an angle.

Use only your best handwriting on a flip chart. If it is still bad, have your charts pre-designed, or get a partner who has great handwriting. The author has a partner with wonderful penmanship whom she calls on frequently to serve "scribe" duty. He does it graciously, freeing the author to maintain eye contact and rapport with the audience.

Tips for Recording Remarks

- Use large type or letters. Write clearly.
- Be sure the information is accurate.
- Use all uppercase or all lowercase letters; do not mix.
- Limit the number of ideas per chart.
- Write, taking notes in pencil on flip charts.
- Change colors for visual relief.
- Underline for clarity.
- Star, box or circle for emphasis.
- Sometimes cover slide or transparency and expose one idea at a time.
- Do not read what is on the visual. Explain, amplify or give examples instead.
- Provide copies of slides or transparencies to participants.

Let Color Do the Walking

If you are using a series of charts, think about color-coding each topic. Next, put masking tape on the side of the flip chart so that you will have a ''tab'' to grab the flip chart to turn it. You will know that you have finished one series of information because of the color you used on the lettering and the strategic locations of the tabs. Remember, the chart is useful for displaying presentation objectives; place it to one side of the room where it will remain in sight for the audience yet not be a distraction.

(**Hint:** If you plan to present information in lists, tape together two color markers, for example red and green. Then as you write, alternate the colors.)

Using Written Materials

If you are going to provide comprehensive handouts about your presentation, tell people ahead of time so that they are not pained with taking copious notes. If the audience knows you will provide notes, they are more apt to sit back and enjoy your presentation.

Handouts must have page numbers. Also, consider differentiating the topic, inputs or segments by using colored paper or tabs; make it easy for the audience to locate the appropriate material and to follow along with you.

Handing Out Material—Timing

Never give out handouts before your presentation unless it is necessary for the audience to follow along with you. The problem with early distribution is that some members of the audience will always read ahead and, therefore, ask questions out of sync or sit back with a bored stare.

USING VIDEOTAPE: CUEING YOUR POINTS

A videotape is a great tool to enhance, explain or emphasize a point. The traditional use of a videotape is to show the tape from the beginning to the end, including the credits! Let's look at the old style, and at a new twist—the video bite.

► **Cueing:** Whichever style you use, have the videotape set up and ready to run before the session begins. A little time spent on this task can save you from a disruptive and embarrassing search for the "selected segment" or from equipment failure.

► **Framing:** Once you have selected your videotape, or a segment of it, check that you can briefly describe the content, and note any key concepts or illustrations that you want the audience to observe particularly. The process to follow in using videotape is:

Introduce the videotape. Briefly describe what will happen. Next, explain why you have selected this particular videotape. Then, list (preferably using overheads) the key points you would like the audience to note particularly. Finally, briefly mention any aspects of the videotape that could distract the audience's attention from the basic message (for example, the familiar face of a TV star).

Framing the "Video Bite" Segments

If you need to show several "bites" from the same tape, here are three ways to avoid losing time—and the audience's attention:

1. Always note timing or footage numbers ahead of time! Have an assistant fast-forward to the next segment while you discuss the last one.

2. Put each segment on a separate tape, each cued to start without any blank leader.

3. Edit your tape so that only the segments you will use are on it, back-to-back. Note and follow the numbers so you will not run into the next segment.

DEBRIEFING AFTER A VIDEOTAPE

After showing the videotape, hold a "debriefing" session. Follow these steps:

STEP 1 Use a preplanned strategy to regain the active attention of the audience. Some videotapes promote a somewhat passive learning environment, and the audience might need something to get them active again.

STEP 2 Through questioning, draw from the audience the pertinent points made by the videotape, and list these on a board or other visual aid. Alternatively, ask the audience to write down the key points, so that every participant becomes active.

STEP 3 Show how this theme helps to achieve the objective of the session.

Summary Exercise

Answer the following by filling in the blank. (Check your answers with those at the bottom of the page.)

1. A ________________ is a great tool to enhance your point.
2. Do not give ________________ before your presentation.
3. Use a star, ________________, or circle for emphasis.
4. Theater-style room set-up is best for ________________ groups.
5. Avoid using a ________________ table for your overhead projector.

ANSWERS: 1. videotape; 2. handouts; 3. box; 4. large; 5. small

MEETING AND GREETING: HOW TO GET A LEG UP

At least thirty minutes before the first participants arrive, organize your handout materials, set up your workspace and check your equipment to make sure everything is working. Plan to arrive early for your presentation, and to stay late to make yourself available for questions during breaks and lunch.

Steve Allen has said that every audience has a single, definite character. A group may be composed of several hundred individuals, but it has one personality in a given situation.

The key to finding out the personality or character of your audience is to greet participants as they arrive. Show appreciation for their attending. Express a genuine interest in why they are attending and try to determine their interests and issues. This greeting establishes a connection and provides information that you might use on what issues or questions they are concerned about. You might think this sounds strange; it is not. You are establishing rapport, creating a dialogue, getting to know your audience and making *everyone* feel more relaxed.

William James, a Harvard psychologist, said that the greatest need of every human being is the need for appreciation. As a presenter, recognize that need for appreciation in your participants; this starts with the greeting.

To accommodate the early arrivals, write a simple message on the flip chart such as, "Good morning. We're glad you're here. Help yourself to a cup of coffee. The class will be starting at 9 A.M." Or, if you plan to use an overhead projector, display the same type of information on a transparency.

> *Hint:* If your group is twenty or fewer people who might not know each other, and if you can get a list ahead of time, print up name tags for everyone in BIG LETTERS. This will help you and the group members get to know each other on a more personal basis. Set the example; wear one yourself. And set out a few blanks for unexpected arrivals.

Here are simple and personal techniques for establishing rapport and gathering information about your audience. At the same time these techniques create an informal tone and making each participant feel welcome.

1. APPROACH each person.
2. SHAKE hands.
3. INTRODUCE yourself.
4. ASK his or her name and title.
5. ASK how he or she is doing.
6. RECOGNIZE those that you have met in the past.
7. ASK open-ended questions to determine their mood.

Do a little research on the group even before you arrive. If you cannot hope to reach everyone, try to pick out the "ring-leaders" and the "loner." If your audience is large, you may only have time to meet a dozen or so people, but this should give you a feeling for who they are and what they are likely to respond to.

Establish Your Personality: Everyone Is a Star!

You cannot expect your audience to get excited about your presentation if you are not. Therefore, the FIRST thing you should do to establish your personality is to show genuine enthusiasm for your topic and your audience.

The SECOND thing to do to establish your personality is to make it clear that you encourage the audience to learn from each other. Give people in the class the motivation and a moment or two to meet and socialize. This will help them feel at ease with each other and give you a chance to glance at your notes or practice establishing eye contact.

> *Hint:* Pick out a couple of friendly faces around the room, or people who seem alert and attentive already, and smile at them. This will help you feel "connected."

FIRST FIFTEEN MINUTES: SUCCESS OR FAILURE

The best way to get where you are going is to make a plan for the trip. A presentation is similar to taking a trip. The audience needs to know where they are going, how they are going to get there, and what you expect them to do.

One way to calm the ''fears of the unknown,'' which we all experience in every new situation, is to answer the following questions in your presentation opening:

- ☐ Why am I giving this presentation?
- ☐ What is this presentation about?
- ☐ Who is the audience?
- ☐ Why is the topic important to the audience?
- ☐ What makes the topic important to me, the presenter?
- ☐ How am I going to deliver the material?
- ☐ What expectations do I have from the audience?

By developing your opening remarks around these questions, you will indirectly establish a structure, calm the audience's fears, and establish a degree of direct and honest communication.

Starting is difficult, yet the first few minutes is your window of opportunity to establish your style, and the tone and the tempo of the presentation. The participants will be watching and judging. They want you to succeed and they want you to know what you are doing. To keep your presentation organized, remember to:

Give clear instructions.
Use variety in delivery.
Promote interaction.
Be consistent in thought and word.
Fit your examples to the audience.

Fifteen Things to Avoid in the First Fifteen Minutes

You will probably be anxious during the first few minutes of your presentation. You should write out your opening statements so that you are well prepared and well scripted. Doing this work ahead of time can prevent empty silence while you search around for something ''appropriate'' to say.

If you are not well prepared, you will be prone to slip into one of these fifteen ''deadly don'ts.'' Look over the list. Be alert to the traps.

1. Don't be dogmatic and force your way of thinking; let the audience come around to your way of thinking by promoting a dialogue.
2. Don't twist a participant's statement to fit your need.
3. Don't tell anyone that he or she is wrong; let facts, logic and group opinion do it.
4. Don't tell the group what to do; convince them they should do it.
5. Don't ask obvious, contrived questions; say, ''What's your thought on that . . .?''
6. Don't deliver more material than the audience can absorb.
7. Don't pick on or ridicule a participant.
8. Don't argue with anyone.
9. Don't take sides.
10. Don't talk too much.
11. Don't try to be funny or humorous (especially if you are NOT normally).
12. Don't be an orator.
13. Don't lecture; ask questions.
14. Don't allow the group to waste time.
15. Don't start the presentation off with a complicated task.

BREAKING THE ICE

Why use ice breakers? Ice breakers provide an opportunity to immediately make everyone—including yourself—feel more at ease, allow you to learn about the participants, and break the audience's preoccupation with work or personal issues. They also help to diminish their fear of what is to come in the learning process.

While an ice breaker should be relaxing, it should definitely make a point which is related to the presentation. Never introduce an ice breaker just for the fun of it.

Ice breaker activities give the presenter a chance to settle in and get a feel for the group, but they should also help participants to focus. An ice breaker should serve as a preview of the topic, as well as an introduction as to how the topic will be presented. Here are three examples of ice breakers that you might consider using:

Example 1: Give the participants a quiz to complete as they are waiting for everyone to arrive. The quiz should contain major points relevant to the topic you will cover. Then correct or discuss the quiz.

Example 2: As a preliminary to making some participants do much of the talking, ask participants to turn to the person on their right and interview them briefly so that they might introduce them to the group. The point of having participants interview each other is to accelerate interaction among the group members.

Example 3: Ask for volunteers to jot down on a piece of paper for you one thing about your topic that they would like to have covered in your presentation. Have these passed to the back (if it's a large room) or to the front (if it's a smaller room). Say that you will review them during the break, and begin your presentation.

Remember, ice breakers are activities that give the presenter a chance to settle in and get the feel of the group, as well as help the group feel comfortable about what they are going to do and what they are going to learn.

Hint: Example 3 could be prompted—for early arrivals—by a notice on a visual aid. These ''contributions'' will help the audience feel a part of your presentation. When you quickly glance through them at the break, they will give you a glimpse of how well your content ''fits'' with their interests and expectations. After the break, you can re-gain attention by mentioning one suggestion that you will cover and one to be covered ''next time.''

ESTABLISH THE FOCUS—BE ORGANIZED AND "CHUNK" YOUR TOPIC

Each new audience is a new experience. The first five minutes of your opening sets the tone and tempo for the presentation. To be successful in your first five minutes, you must be organized and focused.

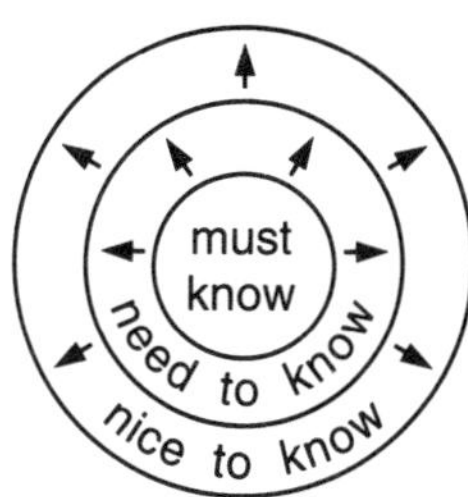

In any presentation, you are likely to have too much material to cover. One way to "chunk" your material down is by using the "minimalist" method. This method suggests that you think of your topic material in three levels of "in-depthness."

The way to do this is to ask yourself: "What is the LEAST somebody attending this presentation would need to know in order for the presentation to be considered successful for that participant?" This step involves several things.

✓ **First,** you should know the need for the presentation, as well as the audience's need. To confirm your understanding of the "need" and to establish your planned focus as appropriate, spend a couple of minutes in the beginning of your presentation finding out the audience's needs. This enables you to pare down the content that you had mapped out, or to elaborate on other areas.

✓ **Second,** write the list of needs on your flip chart and refer to the list each time you cover the point on the chart. By the end of your presentation, manage to cover all the needs listed.

✓ **Third,** try to practice this focusing technique during your design and development stage. Once you get into the habit of "chunking" down a topic to meet the appropriate needs of your audience, you will be able to do this automatically. With enough practice, you will soon see things differently and be able to analyze a situation using your new "chunk circle diagram."

ESTABLISH THE FOCUS (continued)

Survival Tip #2—Getting Ready: Instant Replay

The best way to learn is the simplest. The best presenters know this rule and design and deliver their material in simple, yet specific, chunks of information.

The key to achieving this success is to know your material and to be organized. To present your material in a simple way requires an understanding of the six-step process. This six-step process can be used anywhere, anytime, any place, for anything.

Let me give you an example of how to use the six steps to get ready to present. Fifteen minutes before you are to present, go someplace where you can be alone and have some quiet time. Think through your topic and subtopic, using this structure to develop an appropriate visual map of events, sequencing the material and creating the interactions:

- ☐ **1.** Analyze the task to be learned.
- ☐ **2.** Set the climate for the learning.
- ☐ **3.** Tell the learners how to do the task.
- ☐ **4.** Show the learners how to do the task.
- ☐ **5.** Let the learners do the task themselves.
- ☐ **6.** Review their work in ways that reinforce their achievements and set goals for their improvement.

Believe it or not, this basic six-step process was developed during World War II, when many workers went off to war and their replacements had to learn almost instantly how to carry on production in American factories. Overnight, competence and excellence resulted from using this process.

> *Hint:* The last four steps of the process are usually called Job Instruction Training, or JIT. We often think JIT is used to teach normal tasks such as: tying a shoelace or changing a tire. Yet, JIT works well with mental operations like developing a presentation—try it, you might just like it!

PERSONAL INTRODUCTIONS AND NEEDS ASSESSMENT

Your audience will have many questions that need answers: What kind of presentation will this be (as dull, exciting, disappointing, heavy as the last one)? Who are these other people? Do they know more or less about the topic than I do? Who is the presenter? Is that him/her over there, talking to that other person in the corner? Will I like it here? Will I have to do anything? Where are the restrooms?

Some get-acquainted activities are customary before a presentation starts, but they can be a nuisance to both the presenter and the audience. Try to avoid putting a person on the spot. Remember: they, too, are nervous at the beginning of a presentation.

This is a perfect time for you to conduct an **AUDIENCE NEEDS ASSESSMENT.** The following page lists questions that should be addressed at some point before you begin your presentation.

PERSONAL INTRODUCTIONS AND NEEDS ASSESSMENT (continued)

- ► Who are they? What are their job titles and functions? Are they managers, teachers, physicians? Are they parents, young adults, men, women, older adults?
- ► What do they want to know? Are they eager to listen or are they skeptical? Who is paying for or ordering them to attend? What are they interested in?
- ► What do they not want to know? Have they heard similar presentations recently? Is the topic new to them?
- ► What do they need to know? Are they coming for knowledge or specific skills? If skills, are they job skills, personal skills, career skills or coping skills?
- ► What do they not need to know? How much do they already know about the subject? What will be superfluous or uninteresting to them?
- ► What should you or should you not talk about? What are their backgrounds? What might insult their beliefs or their intelligence? What in your own background might be shared, and what should not be? How can you build your credibility with the group? What are their attitudes?
- ► What are the circumstances? What time of day will it be? What kind of atmosphere? Will people be in a rush to leave at the end? Will they be drifting in and out while you present?
- ► How should you approach this audience? What is your message? How can you best get it across? How can you fit your objectives to your purpose, for this audience?

> *Hint:* Much of this information can, and should, be gathered before you ever meet the group. Call ahead to the sponsors/organizers of your presentation and, if possible, managers and immediate supervisors of the participants.

Use your introduction time to determine some of your audience's needs, but also remember that your audience needs this time to:

- Settle in and feel somewhat at home
- Find out who else is there
- Tell others who they are (show off a bit)
- Have their basic questions answered

Once things settle down, it is time to begin the presentation.

NEEDS ASSESSMENT

Think about an upcoming presentation you will be making, or think back to before the last one you gave. Briefly answer each audience needs assessment question.

1. Who is my audience?

____

2. What do they want to know?

____

3. Are they required/voluntary attendees?

____

4. Is this topic new to them?

____

5. Are they coming for knowledge or specific skills?

____

6. How much do they already know about the subject?

____

7. How can you build your credibility with the group?

____

8. What time of the day will it be?

____

9. What is your message?

____

10. How should you approach this audience?

____

Survival Tip #3—Learning Contract for the Adult Learner

Adult learners come to your presentations with a history. Each participant has an educational, personal and working history. They have also developed a mental contract about your performance, as well as their own performance. Your part of the contract is to:

1. Have first-hand experience that will contribute to the learning situation.

2. Treat the learner with respect and maturity. Recognize the learner as a unique individual with something to share.

3. Be organized; have a well-defined learning goal, objective and agenda. Make your points transferable to personal or professional life.

4. Establish a learning environment that consists of a high degree of safety, mutual commitment and choice.

The participants' part is to:

5. Want to be active participants in the learning process, so include interactive activities in your design.

6. Be critical of excessive procedural red tape, unprepared presenters, poorly articulated programs, and individuals or processes which interfere with the learning process.

7. Be anxious for individual success. Have a strong need for periodic feedback and encouragement.

CREATING A POSITIVE LEARNING ENVIRONMENT

You may remember from elementary school how we had to line up in straight lines for everything, and were taught what we had to know (or ''teached''— as Seymour Pappart at MIT says). For many of us, this is the learning style we are used to.

Adult learners have a strong need to participate in the process of their own learning. Therefore, include some interactive activities in your presentation design.

If you, as the presenter, want people to do things differently from what they are used to, you must provide them with many opportunities to be comfortable with new ideas, in a non-threatening environment, with motivation/reasons to change. You must encourage and allow participants to become involved in the learning process.

Adult learners bring a lot of experience to a training situation. You should acknowledge, honor, and draw on that experience whenever possible. Work on establishing a rapport with the audience. Seek out threads of information about them that you can weave into your presentation.

Few of us are born entertainers. Few of us can keep an audience riveted to their seats or carry on a constant repartee while teaching them something. Fortunately, you do not have to! Simply use energy, get participants involved and create opportunities for each one to experience the excitement of learning and trying something new.

Using Humor

Think of using humor as a way to establish a learning environment in which your audience can feel free and open to learning new things. Then they will be willing to take a chance on changing their ways of thinking or acting. If you are to encourage adults to change, they must trust you. Humor can be a great catalyst for establishing this trust.

CREATING A POSITIVE LEARNING ENVIRONMENT (continued)

Humor itself, the kind that produces a genuine laugh, can enhance the learning experience. However, use humor sparingly. Humor should be used in part to make a learning point, and not just to provide comic relief. If you use humor wisely, it will enhance the learning environment and enable participants to derive greater benefit from your presentation.

Natural humor that comes from your own experience is most effective. It will do three things:

1. Make a point convincing and more easily remembered

2. Share a story participants have not heard and may repeat

3. Show the audience that you are human

You do not have to be funny. The audience will appreciate hearing about you and your experience. If you decide to use stories or jokes from outside your experience, make sure they are appropriate for the group. Stories that someone in business would find amusing may not draw a chuckle from a teachers' group. Be sensitive.

> *Hint:* In ''chatting up'' managers and supervisors beforehand, see if they can help you identify a current in-house joke, or a topic of tension and sensitivity—always related to your presentation content—that might be dealt with by using humor.

Every occupation is marked by its own kind of humor. Your stories or jokes do not have to be embellished, embroidered or delivered with an accent. Just be simple, be amusing, and be yourself.

ADMINISTRATIVE ISSUES

Start your presentation with a very brief orientation about starting and ending times, breaks, telephone calls and messages.

Here is an effective process:

✓ State the objectives of the presentation, timing and agenda.

✓ Get the audience acquainted with the materials to be used; for example, explain that the workbook is theirs to keep and to write in, and that each topic will be summarized on overheads and handouts.

✓ Provide an overview of the presentation, topic and subtopic, methodology and the rationale for your organization of the material.

✓ Address the expectations of the participants which include assignments and level of participation.

By providing this information up front, you avoid forcing your audience to make the big jump from gathering housekeeping information to becoming active participants; the transition should be a natural link in the pace and flow of the presentation.

Timing: Beginning, Ending and Breaks

The agenda is a contract with your audience. The beginning, ending and break times specify the terms. Uphold your end of the contract by firmly establishing the ground rules. Make sure everyone understands the rules and make sure that you and the audience can live with them. For example, if the group is to be back on time, don't you be late.

Publish and announce the times for breaks and specify that these will be the times available for picking up messages and returning calls.

ADMINISTRATIVE ISSUES (continued)

Occasionally you will have trouble with participants arriving late. Try these ideas:

1. Announce unusual starting times: 8:17 or 9:01. It cues the audience that you will probably start when you say you are going to start.

2. Start on time, with an activity that has value and allows you to integrate newcomers. Do not be a stickler about launching into the body of your presentation at the outset, lest you cover things that cause latecomers to be left out or overwhelmed.

3. Offer a value-added idea immediately after the start of the class. It might be something as simple as a tip sheet offering shortcuts to saving time or a cue card on how to counsel an employee effectively—something that rewards those who are on time and makes latecomers a little sorry for being late.

Telephone Calls

Suggest something interesting like the 500-mile rule—that is, have participants act as if they are 500 miles away from their office. Or hold the presentation in an environment that controls calls, allowing incoming messages at the breaks only. Limit access to phones. Geographically remove participants from normal work areas.

PART

IV

The Use of Visual Aids

DELIVERING THE CONTENT

Scanning the Audience

People learn through each of their five senses to varying degrees. Research has proven that it is possible to learn much more in a given period of time when visual aids are properly used. The proportion of learning that takes place through sight may surprise you:

TASTE	**1%**
TOUCH	**1½%**
SMELL	**3½%**
HEARING	**11%**
SIGHT	**83%**

Scan your audience; develop a sense of the learning preference for each member. Listen to their introductions. Do most describe situations in the form of pictures? Is smell or feeling the predominant word used in their descriptions? Or is the description most focused on sounds?

Visual material is an important aid to retention. If you show, as well as tell, your presentation, your audience is likely to remember much more, much longer.

Percentage of Information Retained

	After 3 hours	**After 3 days**
TELL ONLY	70%	10%
SHOW ONLY	72%	20%
SHOW AND TELL	85%	65%

Approximately 70 percent of Western culture is a visual learning culture; therefore, you should formulate your message using visuals and word pictures. Visual material is an important aid to retention. Visuals are used in presentations to:

- Arouse interest
- Encourage participation
- Prevent misunderstandings
- Persuade
- Focus attention
- Save time
- Reinforce ideas
- Add humor
- Enhance credibility

SELECTING PRESENTATION AIDS

''Presentation aids'' are anything other than words and traditional gestures that a speaker uses to help get the message across to the audience. Aids are just that—aid: they should be used only where your presentation *needs* them.

What Points Need Aids

There are five situations in which you need a presentation aid:

1. **The point is too complex for spoken words alone.**

   In other words, you need an aid if you cannot explain the point with only words and gestures in the time you have been given.

2. **Words evoke different visual images for different people.**

   If the point calls up a visual image for you, you want the audience to ''see'' the same image. Will they? A number of participants will not be able to correctly visualize the differences between, for example, poodle sizes (toy, miniature and standard) without some sort of aid.

3. **A high level of retention is desired.**

   Your objective will tell you this. If you want the audience to ''be able to talk about'' this point or take some action related to it, an aid may be just the thing to really get through to them.

4. **Audience attention needs to be regained.**

   Try to determine how alert your audience is going to be. What will happen before you begin, or after you finish speaking, that might compete? How interested are they in your subject? How long and complex is your talk?

5. **Main and/or supporting points need to be summarized.**

   Are you at a point in the presentation where you want to tie several thoughts together? If so, an aid could help you do so with a lot of emphasis.

The reasons for aids are restated below as questions. Ask each question about each verbal point—main and supporting—in your lecture; if you answer "yes" to any question, list the point on a page headed "POINTS NEEDING AIDS." Later we'll discuss what types of aids you can use.

Is the point too complex for words alone?
Does the point call up different visual images?
Is a high level of retention desired?
Do I need to regain attention here?
Do I need to summarize?

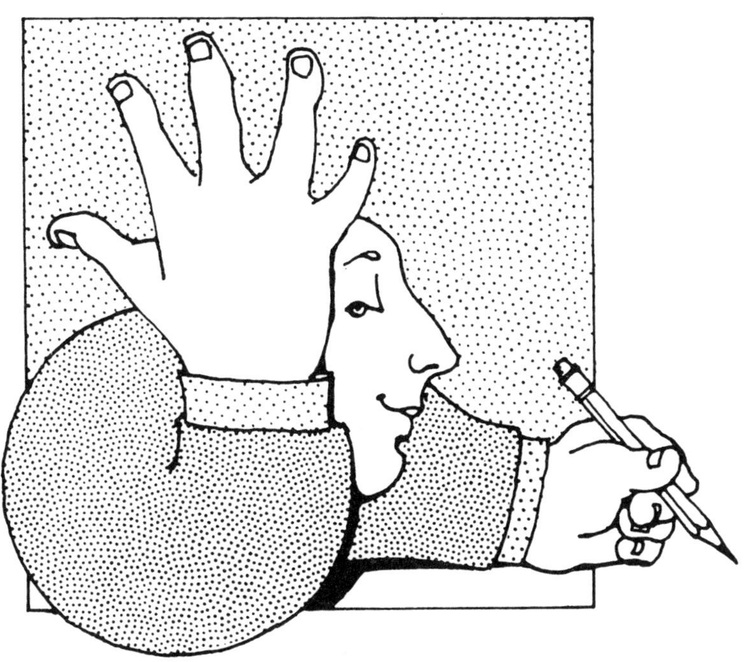

SELECTING PRESENTATION AIDS (continued)

Using Media Effectively

Visual aids are a supplement to your presentation, not a substitute. Their purpose is not to serve as a script or cue cards for you, but as a checklist of key ideas that you will explain, expand upon and emphasize.

The following are effective types of visual aids:

- **Word Charts:** Lists and tables that can be prepared quickly and cheaply by hand or machine. Use the ''seven by seven rule'': no more than seven lines of type; no more than seven words per line. KEEP IT SIMPLE.

- **Organization Charts:** Useful for explaining processes and operations.

- **Cutaways:** A technique that shows aspects of the interior of an object, clarifying spatial arrangements.

- **Maps:** Include only the specific features of land or sea that serve the purpose. Eliminate unnecessary clutter.

- **Graphs:** The LINE GRAPH shows how related sets of facts change according to a common measure of reference, usually time. The PROFILE GRAPH presents the same sort of information, using shading or coloring. The BAR GRAPH compares two facts, but does not show how they change over time.

- **Pie Charts:** Used to show the distribution of percentages of a whole. The circle, or pie, represents the whole, and segments the parts. Make sure that everyone can see the smallest segment. Color the segments you want to emphasize and leave the other segments plain.

- **Chalkboard and Flip Charts:** Best used when you want to build your description step-by-step. They can be used in formal or informal situations. Flip charts are easy and inexpensive to use. There are limits, however, to their effectiveness: they can irritate a group if used too much, and they should not be used at all with an audience larger than 40 people. Always be sure to address your audience, not your chart or the board. We all have a tendency to read material. Do not look at the chart; look at the audience.

- **Projected Aids:** Include slides and transparencies. They are useful for larger groups because everyone can see them. They also give you more control over the image: you can, and should, turn it off when you no longer need it. But bear in mind that projected aids can be too impersonal and distant. Keep them friendly. Use images which are familiar and appropriate. IF YOU CAN USE HUMOR APPROPRIATELY, DO.

He forgot about the "Keep It Simple" rule.

CREATING OVERHEADS

Overhead transparencies are one of the simplest and most effective tools available to any presenter. Numerous studies show that visuals increase the effectiveness of presenting—as measured by retention—anywhere from 38 percent to 200 percent. But as anyone who has ever twisted his or her neck trying to see a washed-out visual from an impossible angle knows, there are "right ways" and "wrong ways" to use overheads.

Interpreting Versus "Reading" Your Overhead

Designed correctly, the overhead can be a highly effective, interactive and inexpensive medium supporting your presentation message. How you present your topic, of course, depends on the audience and your own preference. As a general rule, however, it is best to write your main points on the board or flipchart progressively, expanding each point either verbally or on the overhead. In this way, you keep the most important facts in front of the audience for the whole session. Using this technique, you will avoid the tendency to read the overhead verbatim and, instead, interpret the information for the audience's understanding.

Adding Value to Visuals

One of the best tests of how well you have designed the visual aids for your presentation is whether or not you can present the session without talking. Here are some steps to take to add value to your visuals:

- Use the "seven by seven" rule—no more than seven lines of type, no more than seven words per line. Keep it simple.
- Use only one idea per overhead; do not overload the visual.
- Use color whenever possible, for emphasis.
- Use one style of lettering; either all caps or all small letters.
- Use serif lettering; finish off the "tops" and "bottoms" of your letters.
- Use dark letters on a light background for the text of your presentation; use white letters on dark background for the title and summaries, for emphasis.
- Use color to keep the presentation in sync. Use only a basic color scheme throughout for the presentation; change color to call attention or emphasize a point; use different colors for each segment.

Capturing Attention

If people in the audience can see the visual aid but do not bother to look at it, you might as well not bother to have one. Whatever you use for an aid must:

Catch the attention of the audience

Apply to the audience in some way so that they will keep on looking

Not provoke negative emotional reactions

How does an aid do these things?

1. Attention is commanded by objects and projected devices. People just cannot help looking at them. Do you not find yourself engrossed in movies even if you are not inherently interested in the subject matter? Drawn devices attract attention through color, composition and figures. Your technique of showing the aid will make a difference, too.

2. To apply to the audience, the aid should relate in some way to family, home, job, finances, social status, government or recreation. Look at the following examples on Presentation Aids to see if you can apply them to your own audience.

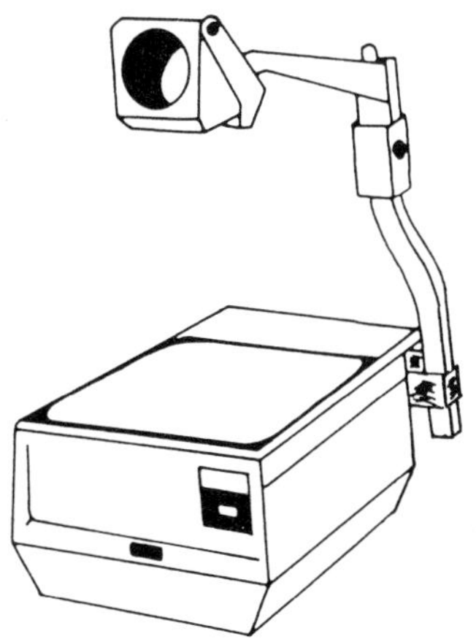

PRESENTATION AIDS

A presentation aid can apply in several ways to the verbal point being made—by clarifying, simplifying, proving, summarizing or emphasizing the point.

Look over the examples shown below to see how they apply to the verbal points they illustrate. One application is given for each aid. Most aids apply to the verbal point in more than one way (the example for ''summarizes'' also ''simplifies'').

Examples

✓ **Not Overdone**
You do not like to be insulted, do you? Nobody else does either. An expert might be insulted by a simplistic view of the subject, but would probably be impressed by the presenter's style of delivering the information in a new way. Never let your aids insult the intelligence of your audience. Eliminate all details that are not essential to the point you are illustrating.

✓ **Visible**
It is annoying to be able to see, but not to be able to read, what is on the presentation aid. Aids should be for the audience, not the presenter. Unseen aids are worse than useless; they are annoying and distracting. Try out all your visuals ahead of time in the room where you will be speaking. Remember to check for adequate lighting, too.

Minimum requirements:

- Symbols (letters): 1/4-inch high for every 8 feet of viewing distance
- Space between lines: 1-1/2 times symbol height
- Screen width: 1/6 the distance between screen and farthest viewer

> *Hint:* Aids usually must be elevated for the audience to see them, especially if the room is crowded.

✓ **Technically Correct**
Obviously you do not want errors in your aid. Or do you? You might want ''errors'' to illustrate the right and wrong ways of doing something. BEWARE of letting the wrong kind of errors slip into your aids, because then you ''inform'' the audience of wrong things—and errors are ALWAYS remembered!

ACCEPTABLE errors: outdated customs or styles, errors the presenter wants to illustrate, and errors that will not mislead the audience

UNACCEPTABLE errors: incorrect or changed procedures, mathematical errors, and incorrect facts (except as noted above)

✓ **Containing One Idea**

Any one aid may seem to contain many ideas—all according to how the viewer classifies things.

An aid should contain only one overall idea, BUT the acceptable number of ''sub-ideas'' contained can be increased as the level of the audience is raised. If a layman has been ''brought to a higher level'' by your talk, you can consider this aid as having only one idea for him or her, too. Base your decision on how much the audience knows at that point in the lecture.

✓ **Suitable for the Occasion**

You surely do not want to use medical terminology in an aid for a group of Boy Scouts—nor would you use layman language in an aid for a group of physicians.

The aid should fit the audience in technical content and the occasion in formality. A good example of this is a group of flip charts that the author created for a listening course for the General Electric Company. She drew figures talking to one another, a simple drawing, but their heads were GE light bulbs. The group loved it because it reflected the corporate culture.

In a formal presentation for the corporate group, using the funny light bulb heads would not be appropriate. Remember to establish context—be appropriate for the environment—and act or perform appropriately.

✓ **Physically Fit**

A speaker once used as an aid a drawing of a balance with too much weight on one side. The drawing was taped to an easel, but in the middle of the presentation it fell, just like the one pictured below it. The contents of the aid made the audience wonder—did the presenter really intend for it to fall to emphasize the point of imbalance?

✓ **Simple and Functional**

Do not let your aids confuse the audience. Each aid should help them. Fancy lettering, complex technology, and pretty little pictures for the sake of pretty pictures are all confusing—be neat and precise. You want your audience's eyes on the visual.

Summaries should be key words, not complete sentences. The aid should be an aid, not a display of creative talent or a crutch.

PRESENTATION AIDS (continued)

✓ **Fit Aids into Outline**
Once you have decided on the aids for your presentation, you must do three things:

1. Every visual needs a verbal setting. First, state what the visual is intended to show, then point out its main features.
2. Integrate your visuals into your script, and rehearse them exactly as you plan to present them. Do not show a visual until you are ready to talk about it and as soon as you are finished, put it out of sight.
3. Make sure you will be able to handle all your aids. Will you have enough time to remove them when it is over? Will you be able to display them during the presentation without help?

> *Hint:* Two final reminders about visuals—the KISS principle and the KILL principle. ''Keep It Simple and Succinct'' and ''Keep It Large and Legible.''

Review

Answer the following by filling in the blanks.

1. It is important to ____________ the overhead; you should not ____________ it.
2. You should use no more than ____________ lines of type, and no more than ____________ words per line.
3. Use ____________ idea(s) per overhead.
4. The visual aids you use must ____________ to the audience.
5. Aids should be for the ____________, not the ____________.

> ANSWERS: 1. interpret, read; 2. 7,7; 3. one; 4. apply; 5. audience, presenter

PREPARE EMERGENCY AIDS

Feel pretty confident about the body of your presentation now? Well, do not feel too confident. There is one thing that has not been taken care of yet—the emergency that you are sure will not happen to you. To somebody else, maybe, but not to you.

Do not fool yourself. Maybe you have been lucky and never had your easel fall over, the screen get stuck halfway down, your assistant get sick, the slide-projector bulb blow out, or Mr. So-and-So change class rooms on you at the last minute. But it could happen. It happens regularly, and sooner or later your turn will come.

So, make it a picnic instead of a panic. All that you need is a little more planning, just in case. After all the effort you have put into your presentation, you certainly do not want it to flop just because of an accident.

The best way to plan for substituting is simply to list all of your aids and then decide how to present the same information in another way—either by talking about the information, by actually sketching the pictorial contents of the aid, or by a combination of the two. Be sure to list all the additional equipment you will need. You can consolidate your plans on the Planning Work Sheet. (See Appendix)

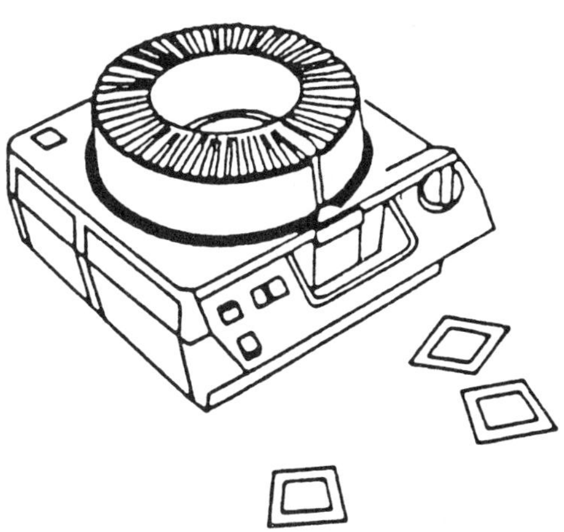

PART

V

Managing the Show

YOU ARE IN CHARGE! ENCOURAGING INTERACTION

Audiences have a variety of reasons for asking questions. Do not assume that they are all seeking information. People may want to test you, to show their own knowledge, to make their own points or to get your approval. Your ability to handle questions and questioners is very important to the overall success of your presentation.

► Receive all questions in an open, friendly manner. Do not over-react or get defensive, even if someone is trying to put you on the spot.

► Listen carefully and restate the question to make sure you understand it and that the entire audience hears it.

► Think before answering. Consider:

1. Why is this question being asked?
2. How does this question fit with my topic?
3. How can I answer as briefly and as well as possible?

► Use the KISS principle: Keep It Simple and Succinct. Do not answer with just ''yes'' or ''no,'' but with a short, to-the-point statement, perhaps supported by a brief example.

► If you do not know the answer, say so. Offer to find out the answer and to get back to the person.

Cross-Discussion

Dr. Israel Scheffler, an internationally recognized philosopher at Harvard University, tells each class, ''You don't know what you know, until you say it.'' Your audience will process information much more effectively and efficiently if you ask the group periodically to speak out, to cross-discuss with you and other members of the group.

There are a number of things that you can do to encourage cross-discussion:

- Ask a question, pause for five seconds and then ask for a response. Often audiences give non-verbal hints that they are ready to respond.
- React to ''false'' answers with acceptance, even if you do not agree with them. Use probing questions to refocus on the discussion topic.
- Encourage silent members to comment, if you think they might have the answer, but are reluctant to speak up: ''This is something you know quite a bit about, Paul. . . .''
- Pick out certain elements of the response and refocus the group's attention on them.
- Try not to answer your own questions too often. After a while you will be performing a one-person show.

OPEN-ENDED VERSUS CLOSED-ENDED QUESTIONS

Questioning is an important basic skill. Good questions make the difference between a passive audience learning poorly and an active audience learning effectively. Questioning is a particularly appropriate technique when you are working with mature learners, who often bring to a program useful skills and/or information that they are willing to share if you encourage them.

Questions are usually divided into two broad categories that form a continuum from open to closed and from general to specific. Whether a question is open or closed depends on how wide the area is from which the participant can answer.

Generally, a closed-ended question calls for a one word response. An open-ended question calls for an explanation. A specific question means that there is one answer or piece of data that is the correct answer. For a general question, a range of answers is possible. An example is the difference between a "true-false" examination and an "essay" examination.

RECALL VERSUS THINKING QUESTIONS

Asking good questions of the audience can also motivate them to learn. In school we were asked a lot of questions, but many of them required only the recall of facts. Facts are important. They serve as the building block to knowledge. Yet, as you may remember, there was a tendency to overdo questions that were only at the recall level. You might improve your questioning and eliminate the one-way monologue by looking at this diagram.

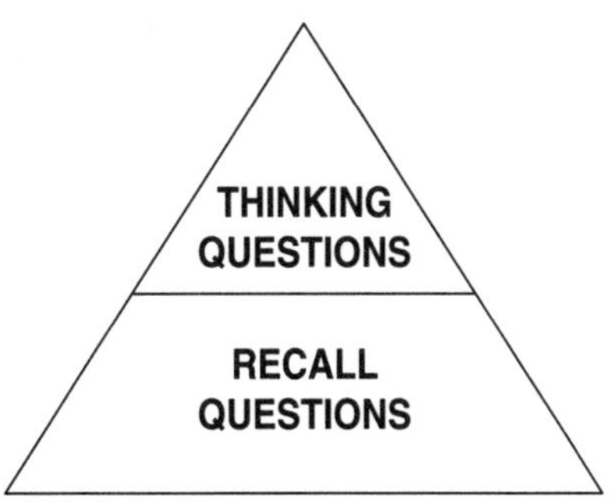

Thinking questions are more provocative than recall questions. They require the audience to put their brain in gear. They ask them to "make a guess," compare, judge, put together, or apply. Here are some examples of thinking questions and recall questions:

Thinking	**Recall**
What would happen if we gave everyone the same rating on performance appraisals?	What is the rating scale you use?
How could we find out the best process for evaluating?	Do all supervisors receive an average rating?

A good mix of thinking and recall questions helps you motivate your audience to become engaged; it also encourages interaction. Emphasizing just recall questions will simply teach the participants that, for example, supervision is a collection of facts, when it is, in reality, far more than that.

Survival Tip #4—Session Planning Format

How to Lead a Discussion

A discussion is an open forum that requires a leader and some planning. For the best results, a discussion period should be a planned segment, and not an occurrence that you let happen because you have not properly planned your presentation.

A discussion is also a technique that you should use to achieve a specific training objective. You use it to promote learning, not to relieve the tedium of other training techniques.

There are three types of discussion plans:

1. Content-focus
2. Broad-focus
3. Strategy-focus

► *Content-focus:* This format is used when you have a specific piece of material that you want to present. You keep the discussion confined to the content and encourage clear understanding of that specific issue; you discourage any abstract leaps. During preparation, develop a specific, achievable objective for this discussion, and each discussion to use as guideposts for arriving at your set outcome.

► *Broad-focus:* This format is for the presenter who is confident in leader-directed skills, one where you develop the art of asking appropriate questions. Your discussion plan will usually be less detailed, but should include a training objective. Develop timing and sketch out your introduction and your conclusion in a detailed outline. Establish your topic area and allow the content to emerge—this is your discussion time!

► *Strategy-focus:* This format is used for learning-discovered learning. The actual content of the discussion receives little planning; what you do plan is the PROCESS of the discussion to create a total experience for the participants. To use this design you should understand and be able to use principles of group dynamics and appropriate questioning techniques. Instead of planning your discussion in terms of minutes, use blocks of time. For example, allow fifteen minutes for understanding the principle or theory and the last fifteen minutes for examples, review and application back to the job.

AVOIDING FATAL FLAWS

There is no one right way to get your audience to work with you, but there are some strong arguments for putting self-directed elements into the presentation.

Individuals like to have control over their own learning. You should design structures and processes that give them increasing responsibility for their learning within the program. It would be a **fatal flaw** to take complete charge of the audience by conducting a monologue, with no opportunity for interaction and feedback.

Another **fatal flaw** is talking about the politics of the company, or about an individual or a policy. Never refer to this type of data. If asked to give your opinion, respond by saying, ''My opinion on this subject is never give an opinion!''

Choose Your Words Carefully

Words can be simple; they can be merely labels. Your name means you; the word ''table'' means a certain piece of furniture. A word produces an image in the audience's mind of the object named. Use words that are as concrete as possible to make your audience see, hear, feel, smell or taste what you mean. Do not say ''creature'' if you mean horse, human or shark. Do not say ''more-or-less''; tell them exactly.

Words are often complex, carrying more than one possible meaning. And sometimes labels are misleading. Remember, most words are only close approximations of true meanings. Rarely does a word tell the whole story. Make your explanations as clear and thorough as possible.

Words are sometimes loaded. Because of the image a certain word may produce in the minds of your audience, you must be careful to avoid provoking strong reactions to words that to you may seem perfectly innocent. Words sometimes have emotional tags attached to them; you must be very sensitive to your group.

AVOIDING FATAL FLAWS (continued)

Never-to-Use Phrases

Never put anyone down for asking a question, even if the question is not very good. Put-downs only make enemies. Besides, your impatience with a question may be based on the risky assumption that you have clearly presented your previous information. Therefore, do not say something like: **"You don't understand what I have just explained?"** Or, **"What don't you get?"**

You can sometimes insult your audience without realizing it, by making an unintentionally hurtful comment. Suppose someone asks a question and you say, **"Well, I thought I explained that, but I'll go over it again for you."**

The never-to-use phrases are setups that can create tension: the audience versus the trainer. Your language should be on the careful side of good conversation.

Remarks

We all have opinions about things. These opinions often fall in the "off-hand remark" category. Your audience will have incredible trust in you, as a presenter, and in what you say. Therefore, remarks which limit are unsubstantiated opinions or "off-hand" remarks.

Sarcasm

Sarcastic remarks are usually not made with a positive intent and are not based on fact but on supposition. Sarcasm as a strategy is unbecoming and biased. You are a facilitator and not a commentator, try to remain neutral. (Do not indulge in sarcasm or make remarks that you would not wish to see in print.)

FOCUSING ON YOUR AUDIENCE

If your audience is relatively unfamiliar with the material you are to present:

- Use clear visuals.
- Emphasize key points and review them using different words.
- Summarize frequently.
- Allow a lot of audience participation. Encourage questions.
- Go from the known to the unknown. Start with where they are, what they know, and then move into material that may be less familiar.
- Be sure to illustrate. For key points, you may need two to three illustrations to really drive home the point. Use clear, simple sentences.
- Think realistically about what you can accomplish in the available time.
- Be aware of information overload.

If your audience has some understanding of the subject:

- Assess your audience in terms of what they know; use this as a frame of reference.
- Be sure to get feedback so you are sure of the level of comprehension.
- Be a gaps person. In other words, you do not have to cover everything—just be careful to fill in the gaps in the participants' information and knowledge.
- Eliminate complex discussions unless they are critical to your participants' understanding.

The experience level of the audience determines the pace and amount of information you present. One sure way to lose the attention of your audience in the first few minutes is to gear inappropriately the level of the presentation to either overspeak or underspeak. Here are some suggestions to help you.

FOCUSING ON YOUR AUDIENCE (continued)

ESTABLISHING THE PACE

The energy level of your audience will fluctuate, and those variations should, to some extent, dictate the methods you use and the content you cover.

Here are some generally accepted guidelines:

✓ Early morning is the best time for you to use a short, quick, punchy delivery.

✓ Midmorning is an optimal time for group involvement activities.

✓ Late morning is a good spot for the tough stuff—it is when people are most alert.

✓ Following lunch, involvement helps to re-energize and overcome post-lunch lethargy.

SMALL-GROUP WORK

When designing projects, doing case studies, initiating role playing and participating in other small group activities, a common question is, ''What size should the groups be?'' The answer depends on what you would like to accomplish from the exercise. (See the Appendix for examples of a case study and a role play exercise.)

A group of two emphasizes team-work and helps people see the value of multiple input.

A group of three is the bare minimum for brainstorming. The triad training design assumes that one person plays the role of supervisor, the next the role of subordinate, and the third person becomes the observer. The subordinate performs whatever task is required and then self-critiques his or her performance. The supervisor then provides additional feedback based on his or her observation. The observer's role is to provide feedback on how effectively the supervisor coached or counseled. Each person cycles through all three roles. The benefits of using a triad design are three reviews of the material, each time from a slightly different perspective, which serves to keep interest high.

If you use **triad** training, you might consider expanding to a group of four, having all four rotate through each role. For example, if you chose to teach a certain skill, the group can teach the skill to the fourth participant as the learner.

Any group larger than seven begins to lose its effectiveness for the purpose of group work. When assigning a task to a group, make sure the group understands the task, the instructions and the time requirements.

GIVING ASSIGNMENTS

Small-group activities seem to lose their punch when some groups finish more quickly than others. You can avoid those awkward gaps in your program with a simple strategy:

> Decide how much must be accomplished to fulfill the goals of the activity. For example, if there are six problems to be solved, it may be acceptable to have three of the six solved.

This strategy will keep your faster groups fully involved, and even your slower groups will probably complete three of the six problems.

> *Hint:* People retain and accomplish more when dealing with tasks they are not allowed to complete as opposed to those they are allowed to complete. We are conditioned to complete things. It creates discomfort when we can't, but that discomfort also has a memory value.

OBSERVATION

A great deal of information is lost because you cannot possibly see and hear everything that is going on. Nonetheless, you can still manage to gather enough information to make some judgment about how well things are going. Let your eyes and ears take in as much as they can. Walk around. Be an active observer. You need to be on your feet roaming around the room, seeing (not looking), listening (not hearing). You must think of yourself as an information gatherer, getting through your senses answers to specific questions. Place a checkmark in each box when you have asked yourself these important questions:

- ☐ How are they doing?
- ☐ What are they learning?
- ☐ What are they struggling with?
- ☐ Do they like the information?
- ☐ Is the information useful (understandable)?
- ☐ Are they making links back to the job?

The key to successful observing is your active involvement in the topic and with each individual in the audience, along with focusing upon providing answers to specific questions.

FOCUSING ON YOUR AUDIENCE (continued)

REGAINING CONTROL

This book encourages you as a presenter to develop and follow a carefully designed plan that is learner directed, and to be a facilitator, rather than a tyrannical lecturer. While it is important to be responsive to audience needs—which may mean pausing from your plan now and again—you are responsible for presenting a certain amount of information in a given time. This means that, unless your presentation is totally inappropriate (which it should not be if you're properly prepared), you should tactfully relegate troublesome individuals, or major group concerns that are really side issues, to a discussion during break or after your presentation.

NEUTRALIZING PROBLEMS

One way to increase audience involvement is to allow time for questions. You should encourage your audience to ask questions. Questions might be slow in coming, but once they do start coming the following suggestions might increase your effectiveness in answering the questions posed by the heckler, the hostile participant, and the competitor:

1. LISTEN to the substance of the question. Do not zero in on irrelevant details; look for the big picture—the basic, overall concern that is being expressed. If you are not really sure what the substance of a question is, ask the questioner to paraphrase it. Do not be afraid to let the questioners do their share of the work.

2. PARAPHRASE confusing questions. You can paraphrase the question or issue in just a few words: ''If I understand your question or issue, you are saying . . . Is that right?''

3. AVOID defensive reactions to questions. Even if the questioner seems to be calling you a liar or stupid or biased, try to listen to the substance of the question and not to the possible personality attack.

Also, remember to check the questioner's comprehension of your answer. Sometimes you can simply check nonverbal cues. For example, if the person seems at all confused, you can ask, ''Does that answer your question?'' Audience involvement and understanding is important for your success.

You may wish to take a follow-up question if the preceding one was relevant to your topic and if it might further clarify the point for others. Two are probably enough, and you should then tactfully return to your presentation plan.

GROUPTHINK

If participants establish a need for learning at the beginning of the presentation, they will be less likely to buy into a *groupthink* situation; they will be more apt to exercise control of their destiny and depend less on the group. One technique for establishing individual ownership and responsibility is to begin the session or program with a needs assessment. This consists of surveying the group to determine their individual needs and then recording them on a flipchart.

Participants may come with preconceived ideas and biases. Most of our attitudes are set. We view learning as easy or hard, important or unimportant. We have attitudes based on past experiences in other learning situations. This is one more reason why the practicality of what is being learned must be stressed. Remember that people do not argue with their own data. Provide plenty of opportunities for people to express what they are learning and how it applies on the job.

Feedback from participants is far more persuasive to other participants than what you, the presenter, say. After all, you have to believe it—you are presenting it.

Each time you conduct an activity that was listed as an individual or group need, you might want to cross it off the needs' flip chart. At the end of the program, review the needs' chart as part of your closing remarks.

FIGHT OR FLIGHT

Occasionally you will encounter a participant who disagrees with you and/or with other members of your audience. To handle this situation, first try to see the "fight chart" viewpoint; listen for understanding. Determine the content of the message, as well as the feeling attached to the issue. Your response must be appropriate, calm and rational to avoid what is called the "escalation effect."

Try to provide an answer which is acceptable, and if necessary, say you will continue the conversation during the break. Do not subject the entire group to one person's agenda if it is not a logical point to be made concerning your topic.

On a different note, occasionally participants come to a presentation with a rebellious attitude. They have either an "I'm here, don't bother me," or a "Try and teach me" attitude. Try to find out either what interests them the most, or if possible, what is upsetting them.

SUMMARY EXERCISE

TRUE OR FALSE

Check your answers with those at the bottom of the page.

____ 1. Participants may come with preconceived ideas and biases.

____ 2. If your audience is unfamiliar with your material, it is best to put as much information in each visual as possible to aid in their understanding.

____ 3. Be aware of information overload.

____ 4. Late afternoon is the best time to present the tough stuff.

____ 5. Ten is the optimum group size for effective discussions.

____ 6. People retain information best when they are allowed to complete assignments.

____ 7. It is important to check occasionally with the audience to make sure that they understand your presentation.

____ 8. If one person is quarrelsome with you, it is important to continue to address his or her concerns until you are satisfied that your point of view is understood.

____ 9. Groupthink occurs in today's seminars, but does not present any problems to the presenter.

____ 10. Paraphrase questions from the audience if you are not sure that you understand what is being asked.

ANSWERS: 1. T; 2. F; 3. T; 4. F; 5. F; 6. F; 7. T; 8. F; 9. F; 10. T

GETTING—AND KEEPING—THE BALL ROLLING

Let's first talk about what you should do after your introduction.

Now that you are "on," immediately connect with your audience by establishing eye contact with several friendly faces. Smile. Keep your movements and gestures to a minimum during the first few moments you talk; let the audience get used to you.

Take your time starting. Get your notes in the right position, find a stance that is comfortable, and spend about five seconds establishing eye contact with your audience. This pause projects authority and quiet confidence.

Begin to speak at a low pitch, with adequate volume. You should be standing in a position for all to see and hear you. Let your face show good news and interest. Keep your body under control. You may be shaky—the first few minutes are the most nerve-racking—but do not worry about it. You will relax as you get started and warm up.

As you begin, make a remark or two that directly pertains to your audience. Tell them something they did not think you would know about them as a group. Remember, your audience will be interested in you only after you have shown sincere interest in them.

Never apologize or make excuses for anything. Be positive and confident. Your audience wants to believe in you, and you should have nothing to apologize for. If you do not know the answer to a question, say so; offer to check on it, and move on.

MAKING SMOOTH TRANSITIONS

What are smooth transitions? Why are they important? Simply stated, a transition means that the process of moving from the known to the unknown is relatively safe; moving from one new idea to another can be treacherous ground for keeping the audience with you.

Connecting or bridging one module or topic to another can be a challenge, yet maintaining a consistent and logical connection of information is important in the learning process.

Smooth transitions can improve your style and effectiveness. Here are seven transitions that work every time:

1. *Question and Answer.* A natural transition, but consider asking the audience to break into small groups. Ask each group to generate questions, rather than asking questions from the group at large. It increases energy, participation and the quality of the questions.

2. *Physical movement.* You can move from one side of the room to another to indicate a transition. Participants' physical movement can also be used. Rotating groups, sending the group on break, and having the groups move somewhere else to accomplish a task can all be used as physical movement transitions.

3. *Use of media.* If you have not been using any media, use a flip chart. You have made a transition.

4. *Change of media.* You have finished with the flip chart, now use the overhead projector. You have made another transition.

5. *Mini-summary.* Ask the group to break into subgroups and discuss what has been covered so far. Ask each subgroup to identify key points. Rotate from subgroup to subgroup and have each verbalize one key point. When you have finished, you have executed a good review—and another transition.

6. *Refocus.* Sometimes a participant may get the group off-track. You do not want to embarrass the individual, but you do not want to take up any more time, either. A simple, "Before Paul made that comment, what was our general topic?" can get you back on track without embarrassing Paul or taking up more time.

7. *Pause.* Silence can be an effective transition.

Survival Tip #5—Transitions

Learning can occur before the presentation starts. Therefore, think about starting activities before the program begins, during lunch and the first few minutes before and after the major presentation. The activities should be fun, loose in format and highly participative.

Some activities that work well are: puzzles with fill-in the blanks; large pictures with a theme, to be colored and titled; a treasure hunt; or a continuous movie, videotape cartoon or just plain classical music playing on low volume.

The objective of these transitions is to break participant preoccupation—to force interruption of things that they may be thinking of, or to alleviate fear they might have about their expected performance in the session.

Introducing the session with a pre-session jump-start seems to make the scary first introductions easier for you, as well as for the participants.

> *Hint:* All participants must address their preoccupation with work and problems, and their anxiety about what is going to happen in the presentation. Help your participants along with this process; introduce a novel, fun pre-program. Also be supportive and ORGANIZED.

BODY LANGUAGE

Your audience will take on the emotions you project. If your face shows joy, they will begin to feel joyful. If you look unpleasant or fearful, your audience will reflect that.

Personality is best shown with a slight smile. If the situation calls for a broader smile, go ahead. Your audience will feel more inclined to like you if you smile.

However, make your expression appropriate to the subject and the moment. Do not smile if you are talking about a tragedy or making a demand.

Check your facial expression to make sure it is:

Animated, not deadpan

Friendly, not off-putting

Genuine and natural, not artificial

Appropriate to your message

Throughout your presentation, maintain eye contact with the entire group. Be careful not to focus on just a few people or on one side of the room, to the exclusion of the other. At all times, your eye contact should:

✓ Be natural and smooth, not forced and artificial

✓ Follow no set pattern

Eye contact is your most potent body language. The simple act of looking a person squarely in the eye is more persuasive than a hundred words.

Do not simply scan the training group and return your eyes to your notes. Look at one person and hold eye contact until you get a response; then pick another person. Keep doing this, and focus on people all around the room. Pick friendly faces at first. Later, after you have warmed up and your audience is with you, you can focus on skeptics and try to win them over.

There is, however, one temptation you must resist. You may feel others have let you down. For instance, if a visual you had ordered did not turn out as you wanted, do not let the audience in on all the details of your unfulfilled expectations. That would be distracting. Just resolve to coordinate things better in the future and keep the audience out of it.

This is finally where it all comes together: your knowledge, authority, concern and confidence are communicated to your audience through your appearance, eyes, face, gestures, voice and, finally, the content of your presentation.

Albert Mehrabian of Silent Messages breaks down the communication impact into results from what an audience sees (visual), how the message sounds (vocal), and the content of the message (verbal). He says that the relative proportions are as follows:

- **The verbal message**—the content—accounts for only 7 percent of what the audience ultimately believes! That means you need help.
- **The vocal message**—how it is said—accounts for 38 percent of what the audience believes. Thus, delivery does count for something. The facts you deliver will not stand on their own.
- **The visual message**—what the audience sees—accounts for a whopping 55 percent of what the audience believes. If you want them to remember what you say, stand tall and say it with pictures.

If you really want to take your presentation seriously, you cannot afford to ignore these statistics. Both Madison Avenue and successful politicians have learned these lessons well. You can too! Be aware of these elements in your visual message:

► POSTURE: Do you look nervous, withdrawn and uncomfortable? Or are you poised, confident, comfortable, erect and relaxed?

► BODY MOVEMENTS: Are you timid, dull, lifeless, awkward or random? Or do you move gracefully, fluidly, with purpose?

► GESTURES: Are they vague, furtive, artificial or wooden? Or are they natural, spontaneous, meaningful, lively, expansive and precise?

TIME CONSIDERATIONS

Running Ahead or Behind Your Audience

Your presentation sets up a dialogue with the audience. Establish your presentation pace but be sensitive to the listening/learning rate of the audience. As they respond to you, make small adjustments in your script and your style of delivery, tailoring it to their responses. It is necessary to establish an appropriate sense of timing and maintain a ''teaching rhythm'' to define your objectives and process, as well as to be appropriate for your audience needs.

If the thing you dread most happens—if the audience seems bored—move faster and risk more, not less. Find a few sympathetic faces and play to them. Raise the dramatic level of your delivery. Care about your audience. Then, if they do not seem to care, think of this as a dress rehearsal and just do the best you can with what you have. What have you got to lose?

Running Ahead or Behind Time

So what happens if you run out of information? Or what happens if you are clearly going to run over? Stop. Then review and take questions. Sense the audience's interest. You might let them share in the decision of whether or not to extend the time and give them a realistic estimate of how much more time will be needed.

Or, you might just quit while you are ahead. Your time limit is a contract between you and your audience—do not spoil your success at the end by breaking it. The only thing more important than starting on time is ending on time.

OVERCOMING AFTER-LUNCH AND 5 O'CLOCK SYNDROMES

Shorter, more frequent breaks may improve the flow of your presentation. If your typical day includes one 15-minute break in the morning and one in the afternoon, consider trying five to seven minute breaks every hour, along with controlled stretch breaks where participants can do stand-up activities.

People tend to feel fresher and more energized if they have taken multiple shorter breaks, as a result of changes in pace and physical position. The use of only one mid-morning break is standard, but not carved in stone. For most participants it is uncomfortable to sit in one place for ninety minutes to two hours with no opportunity to stand up and move around.

Breaks must be logical stopping points in your material. Never break up a module or teaching point because the time has arrived for a break. Plan wisely. Establish discreet presentation modules which are "time sensitive," that is, when breaks occur, they should be natural breaks in the sequence of the information flow. Aim for a module to end before a break.

List two brief activities you have been asked to do by a seminar speaker that you felt were effective pick-me-ups.

1. ____

____

2. ____

____

OVERCOMING AFTER-LUNCH AND 5 O'CLOCK SYNDROMES (continued)

After Lunch

If you are a guest lecturer assigned to the afternoon session, maybe the program director is trying to tell you something. The afternoon is the worst time of the day, and the first fifteen minutes after lunch is your biggest challenge.

There are a couple of reasons why the time after lunch is a tough time for presenting, and your audience might have problems focusing. Here are some common problems:

- Digesting large lunches
- Sense of time is lost—therefore, late arrivals
- All morning material escapes the memory
- Energy levels are at the lowest point

Do not despair. Here are a few pointers:

► Open your afternoon session with energy, enthusiasm and direction. One of the best ways to accomplish this reorientation is to introduce an activity that does two things: reviews the previous material and introduces the new material.

► Design a two-tiered activity. Create small working groups. Assign a problem-solving task for them to work on which they must share with the entire audience. Assign 15 minutes for this group work. After about twelve minutes, tell the groups that they should be ready to present.

► After the presentations, make sure that you tie in their topic with the topic you covered during the previous session, and bridge to the next topic.

► Another simple way to energize the group is to get them to greet each other, to take the time to say hello.

Hint: Never, and I say NEVER, show a movie after lunch. The audience will fall asleep, and you will never be able to re-energize them! The best use of the first couple of minutes after lunch is to establish a reconnection between the material and the participants, as well as to preview the things to come.

Closing the Program: Approaching the 5 O'Clock Rush

Emotions can run high at the end of a presentation or training session. Participants usually feel a sense of accomplishment, a bit of relief that they survived and a touch of sadness at leaving their new friends behind.

To manage those last 15 to 30 minutes, consider introducing a highly participative activity. Here are several fun ones:

1. *Making the Diploma*—give the group five minutes to create their own diploma. They can use colored markers and cartoons or be serious. After the five minutes, have each person stand and explain the meaning of his or her creation.

2. *Cheer Section*—divide the large group into groups of four. Assign each group the task of creating a cheer with a time limit of five minutes to think up the cheer and to practice. At the end of the five minutes, have each group perform.

3. *Letter to Self*—ask participants to write letters to themselves highlighting what they have learned and some things they will continue to work on. Make sure that you put together a form for them to use, with a space at the top for free-writing their thoughts. At the bottom of the form, create a box labeled ACTION PLAN for them to record issues and a time frame line.

These are just a few of the activities you could use. The important thing is to be appropriate. If you have had a very active session, introducing an activity might be deadly. Think through your design and use some sense about sequencing events.

Briefly outline an activity you might want to try—be original!

____

____

____

____

____

____

____

____

FINAL CLOSING

All presenters hope to **end** their presentations as they planned. To ensure success, remember the 2 P's:

PLANNING

PACING

Planning—this means having a firm understanding of where you want to be at the end of your presentation and an understanding of each step that you are taking to get there.

Pacing—this means having a sense of rhythm, understanding your natural speaking pattern. Think—do you time pauses? Do you speak fluently or haltingly? Are you too fast or too slow?

> *Hint:* Present single ideas. Plan your content and how you are going to process your information. Do not throw too many ideas at your audience at one time. If you do, most of them will get lost. Encourage participants to react to an idea once you have presented it. And, communicate as accurately as possible. Use examples, analogies, and illustrations. Avoid generalizations. Present difficult things in sequence. Spread out the difficult task with some easy, fun things.

Reviewing and Summarizing

Evaluation is a scary word if we think only in terms of formal reports comparing one presenter's behavior with another. Evaluation is too often used as a weapon instead of a productive, positive way to diagnose the effectiveness of delivery techniques.

Evaluation does not have to be a negative experience if we take the time to develop a few techniques that bring out its positive, productive aspects. Let's consider how to acquire feedback that will help you plan and evaluate your presentation.

TESTS AND QUIZZES

The usefulness of traditional testing procedures is limited. In grade school we all were studying the same thing at the same time; it was easy to administer an evaluation of the learning. To use a test or quiz successfully with your audience, follow this six-step strategy:

- Determine the behavior you want to support or reinforce with the participant.
- Determine the audit method to be used to evaluate progress.
- Develop an audit worksheet.
- Develop performance standards for both the training and on-the-job observation.
- Determine what stops the individual from achieving the performance standards.
- Establish a report mechanism. You might either give participants a call, or send out a progress inquiry note.

Make testing automatic and easy. Constantly recap and/or summarize important points. Do this by either listing the points in your dialogue or having participants list the learning points, finish your sentences or record the points they felt were significant.

FINAL QUESTIONS AND CONCERNS

You will probably have a question and answer session at the end of your presentation. Plan ahead for it, know the answers to questions you are likely to receive, and rehearse. Be prepared to conduct the session as professionally as you performed the rest of your presentation. What happens if you ask for questions and no one responds? When the pause starts to get too long, you have several options:

- Have a colleague or two planted in the audience to get the questions started.
- Ask a question yourself: "Someone once asked me . . ."
- Terminate gracefully, "If you have no questions, we'll finish for today."

FEEDBACK AND EVALUATION FORMS

Jotting down brief notes about participant involvement throughout the presentation can prove valuable later when discussing a participant's progress. Also, the notes you keep can provide accurate information on specific behaviors and skills that the participants' exhibit.

Your attention to detailed information during the presentation can give you data on the content and process of the training so that you can give managers a specific progress report, rather than just general impressions of the whole group.

Consider the evaluation process as an ongoing process, which you should conduct prior to and during the program. It is important for you to evaluate each step of your design and delivery to make sure you have met your individual teaching objectives.

Here are parts of the process that can be critical to a successful transfer of knowledge to your audience:

NEED—The participants, their manager(s) and co-workers come to the conclusion that the training was necessary.

GROUP MIX—The appropriate people attended the program. In other words, the right prerequisites and shared vocabulary were used. Also, comparable opportunities were available to apply the training following the program.

SCHEDULE—It was optimal for learning and on-the-job integration.

OPPORTUNITY—Participants had both the time and the opportunity for on-the-job application immediately after the training.

FEEDBACK—The success of on-the-job application of the training, as well as the program itself is communicated to the organization.

CHECKLIST: Factors you should review during your presentation:

- ☐ Did I *find* at least two friendly faces?
- ☐ Did I *maintain* some eye contact with almost everyone?
- ☐ Did I *check* for audience understanding?
- ☐ Did I *clarify* points that seemed ''fuzzy''?
- ☐ Did I *answer* questions appropriately?
- ☐ Did the exercise(s) *emphasize* an appropriate teaching point?
- ☐ Did the presentation *meet* my established teaching and learning objectives?
- ☐ Did the audience *achieve* an acceptable level of understanding?

THE END

For you, the end is just the beginning. You have worked hard. You have developed some new design techniques and presentation skills.

The ending of this book is the beginning of a new and rewarding experience for you and for your audience. Have fun and remember:

Plan your topic

Prepare your material

Present masterfully!

With this book you automatically become a member of our Trainer-Net. You may call 24-hours a day if you have questions, comments, suggestions or ideas at (703) 435-1182.

PART VI

Appendix

PRESENTATION DEVELOPMENT MODEL

Planning

About the Presentation:

Where: ______________________________

When: Date: ________ Time: ________ Duration: ________

What: Specific topic: ______________________________

____

Purpose (to inform or to persuade): ______________________________

____

Desired Results: The audience will be able to ______________________________

____

Presentation Objectives:

1. ______________________________
2. ______________________________
3. ______________________________

Did you clearly state Purpose, Topic, and Desired Result?

About the Audience:

Who: ______________________________

Number attending: ______________________________

Why they are here: ______________________________

Their knowledge of the topic: ______________________________

Their vocabulary level: ______________________________

PRESENTATION DEVELOPMENT MODEL (continued)

About the Facilities:

Location and directions: ____

____

Seating Arrangement: Draw a diagram below of the presentation room. Where will you place the podium? Your audience? Presentation aids?

Are there any special factors you need to consider? ____________________

____

____

Organize Your Material:

TITLE: ______________________________

TOPIC: ______________________________

APPROACH: ______________________________

____

SEQUENCE: ______________________________

____

METHOD: ______________________________

Presentation Body:

MAIN POINTS AND SUPPORT

Point 1: ______________________________

____

Support: ______________________________

____

Point 2: ______________________________

____

Support: ______________________________

____

PRESENTATION DEVELOPMENT MODEL (continued)

Point 3: ______________________________

____

Support: ______________________________

____

Point 4: ______________________________

____

Support: ______________________________

____

Presentation Aids:

____

____

Are there any other special arrangements or considerations?

____

____

____

____

Preparation

Introduction:

____

____

____

____

____

Conclusion:

____

____

____

____

____

____

Summary:

____

____

____

____

____

____

____

____

____

Number of pages: ______ Number required: ______

THE CASE STUDY

A case study is a description of an event or a problem situation. The description often has some narrative element, together with enough background material to make the problem appear to be "real" and to allow the development of "real" solutions. The description usually has a narrow theme to ensure that the example results in a specific educational outcome. The narrative is often followed by several questions. The case is usually presented in written form. The amount of detail may vary greatly; for example, many case studies involve about one-half of a printed page, but some can be as long as fifty pages. The case study involves some form of debriefing activity, often a small group discussion.

When Should You Use a Case Study?

Use the case study when you think your audience would be motivated by working on a "real" problem. But, use the case study only when you have sufficient time available for discussion of various problem solutions.

> *Hint:* Consider having the participants write their own case study in class. This will provide an opportunity to exchange "real" information, as well as motivate participants to take an active interest in problem solving.

Situation Example:

Mary Jones has been a hard-working, focused employee for approximately six months. Mary has always arrived early and stayed late, and has completed each task accurately and quickly.

During the last couple of days Mary seems to be consistently ten minutes late, has no interest in her job and makes lots of mistakes. You are concerned.

Questions to Ask the Audience:

1. What is going on here?

2. What is the problem?

3. What is your first step?

A discussion based on this case might have the following outline:

1. Establish the past situation.
   a. Arrived on time
   b. Hard-working
   c. Completed her tasks
   d. High degree of accuracy

2. Establish the present situation.
   a. Arrives late
   b. Not focused on the task
   c. Makes mistakes

3. What can be done.
   a. Ignore the situation—it will go away
   b. Discuss the issue with Mary
   c. Ask Mary if she is having some problems that you might talk about
   d. Give her a written warning
   e. Dock her pay

The major advantages of the case study are:

- The process encourages participants to transfer learning into the real world of problems on the job.
- The discussion provides the opportunity to listen to participants' methods of problem solving.
- It encourages an exchange of ideas and opinions.

The major disadvantages of the case study are:

- The case focuses on a single, isolated event which might not reflect the real work situation.
- The participants usually look for a quick solution and do not develop analytical skills or apply the theories that are being taught.
- The participants become somewhat detached from the situation because they do not know the characters personally.

ROLE PLAY

There are two types of role play: preplanned and spontaneous. The preplanned role play is actually a short case study. The difference is that the role play problem is acted out, while the case study problem is presented in narrative form.

To role play, you select one group of participants, assign them roles and give them role descriptions (or briefings). You give the other participants only a background statement. Ask the participants to play clearly detailed roles; they may be quite different from the participants' usual behavior.

The spontaneous role play happens when you give a participant a role in which he or she basically plays himself or herself, but ''tries out'' certain new behaviors to expand his or her range of responses. Spontaneous role plays need minimal role briefings, but require detailed observer's guides.

Situation Example:

Max has recently recovered from open-heart surgery and has been asked to cover the switchboard on Friday, while Mary picks up her child from nursery school.

Today is Monday, and Mary has informed you that she needs to change her lunch time to pick up her daughter at the child care center. Max is the designated back-up. Since Max's surgery, however, he believes that he must exercise every day at noon, because he likes working with a specific instructor. It is a matter of life or death with Max; therefore, he does not want to cover the board at noon.

> **Role: Person A**—Mary says that she needs to leave during the noon hour to pick up her daughter.
>
> **Role: Person B**—Max declares that he will die if he does not exercise every day at noon.
>
> **Role: Person C**—Supervisor must resolve this issue between both employees.

Observation Guide: Look at the verbal and physical behavior exhibited by the characters. Record the strategy the characters use to resolve the problem.

Processing the Role Play:

1. Ask the "actors" how they felt, what they liked or disliked about their performance.

2. Ask individual audience members what their response is.

3. Try to determine the group's resolution to the problem.

Advantages of a role play are:

- The role play is an action-oriented process which allows the participants to practice skills in problem solving. It allows the others the chance to watch a problem being resolved.

- The role play can help the participants to understand the effects of their behavior on other group members.

Disadvantages of a role play are:

- Some people do not like to role play and have a problem with being a participating member—or refuse to participate altogether.

- The situation might be viewed as one-sided and artificial.

- The role play is a time-consuming exercise.

NOTES

NOTES

NOTES

NOTES

NOTES

OVER 150 BOOKS AND 35 VIDEOS AVAILABLE IN THE 50-MINUTE SERIES